EVENTING

JO WINFIELD FBHS

THE CROWOOD PRESS

First published in 2011 by
The Crowood Press Ltd
Ramsbury, Marlborough
Wiltshire SN8 2HR

www.crowood.com

British Library Cataloguing-in-Publication Data
A catalogue record for this book is available from the British Library.

ISBN 978 1 84797 301 6

Disclaimer
The author and publisher do not accept any responsibility in any manner whatsoever for any error or omission, or any loss, damage, injury, adverse outcome, or liability of any kind incurred as a result of the use of any of the information contained in this book, or reliance upon it.

Acknowledgements
I would like to thank the following for their help and support: Jane Williams for her photography and encouragement from the start to the finish; Pauline Williams and Sarah Philips for an honest overview of my work; my riders Alice, Tasha, Emma and Kelly, and their horses, without whose help and support I could not have completed the book. I would also like to thank Hartpury College for its excellent facilities, and Tor Brewer for her facilities, owners and wonderful horses.

Illustrations by Claire Colvin

Typeset by Jean Cussons Typesetting, Diss, Norfolk
Printed and bound in Singapore by Craft Print International

Contents

Foreword

Many enthusiastic riders who wish to embark competitively in Eventing need help in the early stages, especially in the purchase of a suitable horse. However, at every level skills and knowledge need to be updated and improved to make progress towards your goal. Within the pages of this book there is a wealth of information, from simple basic skills to more advanced levels. There are many good illustrations, both photos and diagrams, which clarify what is described.

Riding skills are always important, but Jo Winfield explains how other aspects are important and guides the reader in the right direction. For example, rider fitness is not often considered, but it is addressed here and is vital to make the task easier for both horse and rider to avoid unnecessary stress, as an unfit rider can make the horse's task difficult and may cause injuries to both. We all, as competitors, feel there must be a short cut to achieve success, and learn to our misfortune that good basics are invaluable and short cuts don't last. You now have the opportunity to browse through the advice in small doses, rather than have to read it all at once.

This book helps riders to understand the temperament and mechanics of the horse, to train in manageable stages, and enter the right classes for the appropriate level of training. It also highlights the importance of the riders' preparation, both mentally and physically. Eventing is a highly competitive sport where amateurs and professionals compete side by side, as do both men and women. Due to the safety aspect it is important that rider and horse form a partnership in order to minimize risk, and Jo guides you through basic safe practice.

It is possible to enjoy and achieve personal success at all levels, and once you have studied the ground rules and the information offered in this book, you will soon be able to take part in Eventing safely and successfully.

Gillian Watson
MBE, FBHS, Trainer of British Junior and
Young Rider Three Day Event Teams

Introduction

This book has been inspired by my personal philosophy to produce riders who are realistic and can identify their own strengths and weaknesses, and those of their horses, but who can then use this knowledge to achieve success at either a personal or a competitive level. My inspiration is to produce an improved, safer and more successful eventing competitor who can enjoy their horse and their sport. Personally I have competed in one-day and three-day events from grass roots to two star level in British Eventing horse trials, and this book reviews some of the common sense and lessons I have learnt along the way. I hope it will guide you in your preparation for, and when you actually compete at, your first event, and will help you to progress and to achieve your aspirations.

This book also aims to provide an insight into training the novice event horse, including how to prepare for competition and how to improve your competitive performance. This starts with the ability to critically assess your own horse so you can highlight its strengths and weaknesses as an event horse. Being realistic about what your horse is naturally capable of achieving enables you to put together a suitable training plan for all the phases of eventing.

Other key areas addressed include the demands of the competition, what is expected at each level of competition/class, and how to be appropriately prepared, the psychological aspects of competition training, and factors to consider when progressing to the next level. I have deliberately described the 'pros' and 'cons' of both the horses and riders featured throughout the book in order to provide a visual aid to training, and also reassurance that from acknowledging our weaknesses we can turn them into strengths. Many of the exercises are illustrated in a diagram and/or a photo sequence to help you interpret how to apply them in order to improve your own riding or your horse's way of going, and incorporate progressive steps to help you move through the grades.

I hope that whatever your level, you find a hint, tip or exercise that will help make your eventing more successful and, most of all, enjoyable!

Jo Winfield

1 The Ideal Horse, Conformation and Biomechanics

INTRODUCTION TO EVENTING

The modern-day sport of eventing originated as a performance assessment for the military, where the army horses were expected to meet a variety of challenges that demanded control (dressage), speed and endurance (cross-country), and athleticism and overall fitness (show-jumping). Eventing as we know it nowadays became modified as an equestrian sport when it was included in the Stockholm Olympic Games in 1912, although show-jumping was accepted in the 1900 Games. The Fédération Équestre Internationale (FEI) was formed in 1921. Up until 1952, only male cavalry officers could compete in the Olympics; in the 1952 Games both men (civilians) and women were allowed to compete in the three Olympic disciplines. The equestrian sports are among the few Olympic sports in which men and women compete equally against one another. The first regular, British, Olympic-level event was the Badminton Horse Trials. This was first held in 1949, and initially only British riders (male and female) were allowed to compete. It is now open to all riders from around the world who have qualified for this level of competition, along with other four star events such as Burghley, which began in 1961.

Horses have to qualify to compete at all levels, with nations as well as individuals requiring qualification for world class events. These events run over three or more days, but at the lower levels the competition is organized to run over twenty-four hours (a one-day event). In Britain the British Eventing (affiliated) classes begin at grass roots level with BE80, and then progress upwards through the grades classified as BE90, BE100, Novice, Intermediate and Advanced.

THE MODERN SPORTS HORSE

The sports horse has to be able to perform in the three disciplines of dressage, show-jumping and cross-country in a time-scale from one up to three or more days. This is the equivalent in human terms to the triathlon, where a multi-skilled approach is required for three activities carried out in quick succession. The physical and mental skills demanded of the event horse are inevitably varied, but through modern breeding strategies it is possible to produce a specific type of horse suitable for the accomplishment of these skills.

It is generally accepted that the modern day élite event horse must have a high proportion of Thoroughbred breeding, with a small percentage of non-Thoroughbred blood – between $1/4$, $1/8$ or $15/16$ per cent – such as Irish Sports Horse (ISH), Selle Française or warmblood making up the final event horse mix. This amalgam should provide the speed, endurance and temperament required at the higher levels. Whatever the horse's breeding, however, the prime considerations must be its conformation and soundness, and also its temperament, because this reflects its trainability.

For the amateur rider who may be competing

up to Novice or perhaps even at Intermediate level, breeding is rarely the prime factor when deciding to purchase an event horse: conformation and how this links directly to the soundness of the horse has to be the first priority, closely followed by the temperament and trainability of the individual horse. Modern-day lifestyles dictate that the amateur rider often has a full-time job not associated with horses, so that the management of the horse must be provided by means of either DIY stabling or part livery, and its welfare and training need to be fitted around a busy working life: needless to say, balancing all these commitments and responsibilities demands serious attention.

Certainly at the lower levels of both unaffiliated and affiliated eventing the successful event horse comes in all shapes and sizes, since its primary requirement must be to suit the needs of the rider, namely their shape, height and build. Therefore it is important when considering the natural attributes of a horse that its height, size and shape suit the build of the rider. Putting a lightly built lady on to a 17hh heavyweight horse is likely to lead to an issue of control in that she may lack the strength needed to ride this type of horse. On the other hand, if a tall businessman is looking for a horse he will need something with sufficient size and substance to accommodate his weight and height. However, all successful event horses will have the qualities of soundness and good athletic movement, and a reliable temperament that makes them bold and trainable. Almost any type of horse should be capable of competing through to Novice level, so when considering a horse for this standard a very athletic, talented élite event horse is not necessary or even ideal, since such a horse can be very hard to manage and train alongside other non-equine commitments.

The rider's competence should also be considered. A schoolmaster can provide vital experience and an inherited skill set to a rider just starting out, and a horse that knows his job can give a great deal of confidence to someone wishing to step up to another level. With the older horse some consideration should be given to any lumps and bumps that he might have acquired in the course of his competitive years, and other factors such as stiffness and an established way of going may not be ideal; however, a proven competition record should be reassuring as regards soundness and consistency.

If a horse is being purchased as a competition prospect, then a full five star vetting is advisable, and your vet should be informed about the type and level of the events that you hope to compete in, so that he can assess whether the horse is 'fit for purpose'. Depending upon this level and the value of the purchased horse, x-rays may be required of different aspects of the feet, knees and hocks. This will give the new owner an overview of the horse's physical strengths and weaknesses, and the areas that may need to be monitored; it will also provide a veterinary certificate for the purposes of insurance.

THE IDEAL CONFORMATION

The four horses in Figs 1.1–1.4 have, in their different ways, a conformation that makes them suitable for eventing, and indeed they are all competing, or are about to compete, in British Eventing events. These horses are used for the images throughout this book, and it is useful to be able to compare their conformation when standing up in hand with how they appear in movement in the photographs later in the book.

The horse pictured in Fig. 1.1 is a good stamp, with a well proportioned body. His eye is kind and alert, showing interest but also giving the impression that he is quite relaxed. His head is well set on to his neck, allowing plenty of room for flexion when he is asked to

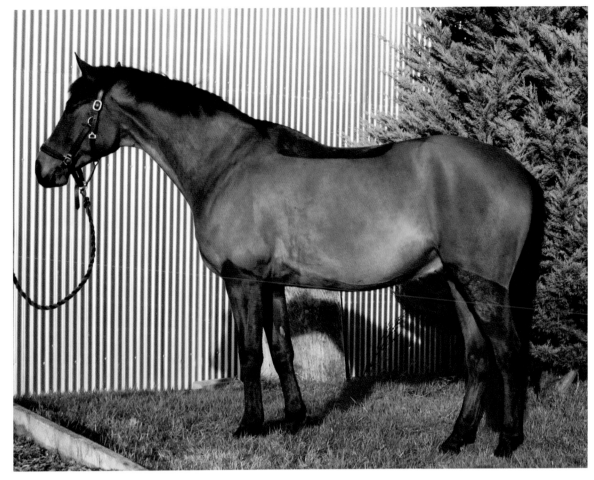

Fig.1.1 *Eleven-year-old 16.2hh Belgian warmblood gelding currently eventing at BE Novice level.*

work 'in an outline'. The shoulder and forehand are well balanced, showing similar shoulder angles to the hoof/pastern axis. The wither is pronounced, but not excessively so, therefore fitting a saddle should not cause problems. His back is in proportion, being neither too long nor too short. The height of the wither and the croup are similar, with the shoulder a little higher, so he will find it relatively easy to maintain a more 'uphill' frame when ridden. The forelimbs are straight, with a shorter cannon bone in proportion to the length of the forearm. The knees are flat, with clearly defined tendons and ligaments. Although in this picture

the horse is not standing square, his weight is evenly distributed over each of the legs.

Being critical, his hind leg is rather weak: although the hamstring muscles are clearly defined, the hindquarters lack development, with the second thigh being less developed. The semitendinous muscle is clearly defined from the tail towards the hock, but it is overdeveloped as a result of the horse pushing away from his weight rather than carrying it. In the image the horse is standing slightly 'out behind': if a line were drawn from the point of the buttock to the floor, the hocks protrude to the right of the line, when they should be aligned with it. From a development point of view this needs improving, first to support the pushing power, and then to enable the horse to work in a more collected frame, as is now required at his level of training and competition.

Almost any type of horse can event at the lower levels providing that his conformation is basically correct, with the limbs being of prime concern; this is important in the event horse if he is to be able to perform in a variety of ground conditions and stay sound, fit and healthy. It is probably impossible to find the perfect event horse by just assessing what he looks like, but it is useful if the 'perfect model'

is considered as a benchmark against the horse that we are looking at with a view to purchase. Thus as we have seen, as a starting point he should be correct in his conformation and in his general appearance. It is an interesting point that a well proportioned horse is often bigger than he looks, his proportions giving him an equality in his body sections unrelated to how big or small he is. And the horse that is evenly balanced in his proportions is often well balanced in movement, being able to place his weight equally through his limbs, with the forehand and hindquarters being of similar height and his weight evenly distributed through his whole body.

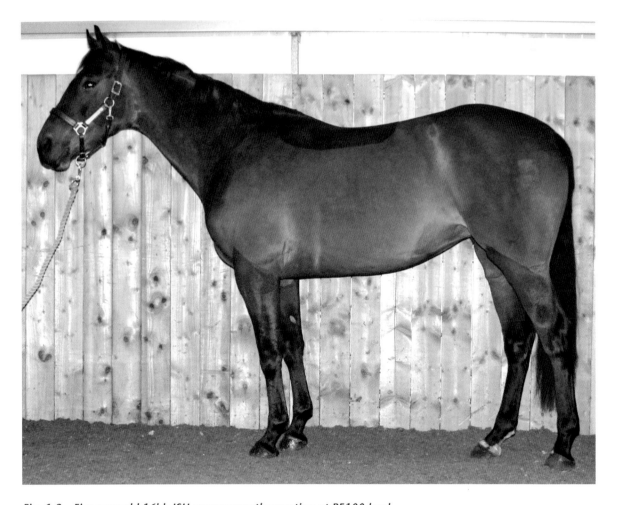

Fig. 1.2   Five-year-old 16hh ISH mare currently eventing at BE100 level.

Fig. 1.3   Five-year-old 16.1hh Dutch warmblood mare currently jumping BSJA Discovery classes.

The mare in Fig. 1.2 has had a good first season eventing and has finished fit and well. She is a middleweight type, with substance from her Irish breeding, though she does lack the blood of a Thoroughbred cross. On first impression she appears to be standing a little lower through her forehand than her quarters, and this may predispose her to riding 'downhill' (being on her forehand). Nevertheless she has well defined hindquarters and second thigh, indicating that she can generate impulsion; however, the lack of development in her topline, and particularly her neck, indicates that

she has not been working in a balanced and 'connected' outline. This might predispose her to jumping with a somewhat hollow shape, which if not corrected might raise concerns regarding her soundness in the long term.

The horse in Fig. 1.3 has an interesting conformation, as she looks very different under saddle compared to when she is stripped and standing in hand. As a five-year-old warmblood she still needs time to mature, which is why she is currently show-jumping and not being subjected to the greater rigours of eventing. She has a kind eye and a lovely nature, but at present lacks some physical development. Although her neck is well set on to the shoulder, it lacks development along the topline (and in particular the trapezius muscle): this lack of development makes the wither look overly prominent at the moment. Her shoulders are well in proportion and she has short cannon bones, compact pasterns and strong feet, which are a matching pair. Her back is rather long and is raised over the lumbar sacral region, which as a result may lack flexion and mobility when she is being ridden. This weakness will predispose to the hind leg lacking strength, and may compromise her ability to take the weight off the forehand.

Fig. 1.4 shows a Russian Trakehner, and the first impression is of how strong this horse is as a type, powerful in his frame throughout his whole body. He is also very inquisitive and alert, his ears constantly twitching as he takes stock of his surroundings – a good characteristic providing it doesn't also mean that he is excessively spooky. His head is well set on to his neck, although his neck lacks some development around the wither, in the trapezius muscle. He is quite short through the back, which will enable him to throw a powerful jump, but he does lack some suppleness, which will show up more in his flatwork and in his ability to take the contact forwards. His legs are compact and well proportioned, with short cannon bones and

Fig 1.4   Ten-year-old 16.1hh Russian Trakehner gelding currently eventing at BE Intermediate level.

clean limbs. He is competing well at Novice level, but would possibly lack some speed for the higher levels.

CONFORMATION AND BIOMECHANICS

Many a horse has been purchased over the stable door as a result of his immediate emotional appeal to his beholder. But whilst it is always gratifying to have an attractive horse, to assess him by his facial appearance, his kind eye and his colour alone is not the most constructive way to make a judgement,

which should be on a logical basis and not a subjective emotional one. Different breeds do have different conformational traits: thus warmbloods often have a very broad forehead and a wide nose, whilst Thoroughbreds tend to be slender and elongated through their brow and nose. Whatever the breed, they should have a kind eye and a generally well proportioned facial structure, but be wary of markings such as stars and blazes, as these can sometimes make the facial features appear offset, which can make the horse itself seem less than straight as he proceeds down the centre line in a dressage test.

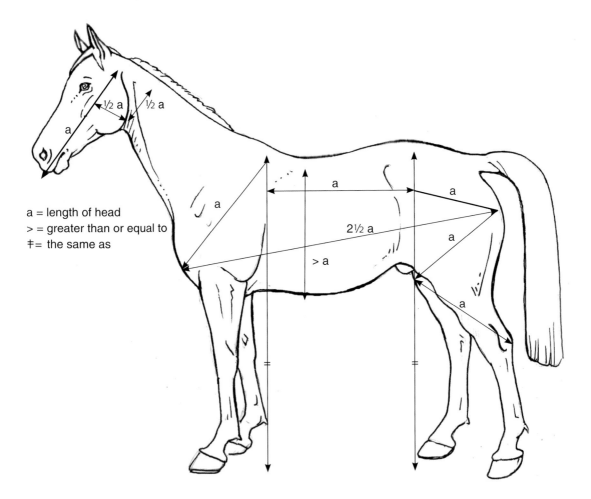

Fig. 1.5   Equine biomechanical proportions.

The Head and Neck

The head and neck should be strong enough to present a good topline without the neck being too short. There should be no restriction through the mandible and jowl area, which could potentially limit the horse's ability to flex through the top of the neck, making it hard for him to work 'on the bit'. Such a restriction through the jaw area might also limit his breathing capacity, so he cannot maximize his oxygen uptake under strenuous exercise. Ideally the jaw at this point should be as wide as a human fist.

The conformation of the mouth should also be considered, in that a thick tongue and small lips can cause bitting problems. The structure and conformation of the teeth should also be assessed, perhaps in the course of a pre-sale vetting or by a dental technician, and any abnormalities identified that might lead to bitting and/or training issues in the future.

When we talk of the horse's conformation, this describes his basic skeletal structure; however, his muscular development can significantly change how he looks – his visual appearance. Thus an over-developed brachiocephalic muscle (the muscle starting at the bottom of the head and running underneath the neck to the base of the chest)

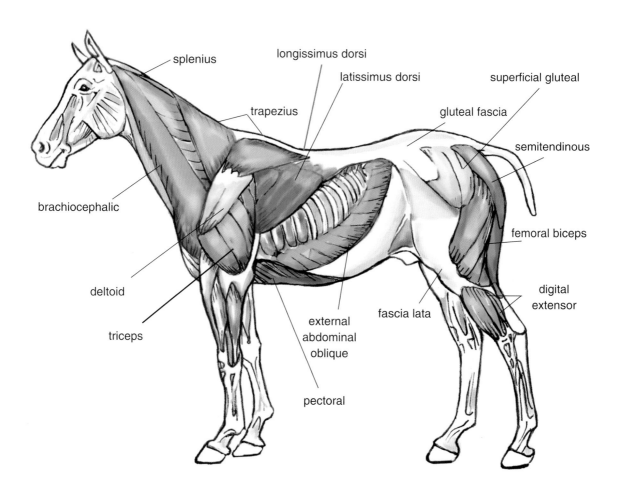

Fig. 1.6 The superficial muscles.

gives the impression that the horse has a short neck with an inverted topline, whilst it is in fact poor development of the 'topline' muscles – the splenius, rhomboid and trapezius muscles – that inhibits the development of his neck and makes it look upside down, rather than his actual conformation.

The Shoulders and Forehand

The shoulders link the neck to the back and their conformation is significant for several reasons. First, the top of the shoulder from the scapula into the wither provides the point of placement for the saddle, the area behind the scapula directly influencing the site and position of the saddle. Thus prominent or alternatively very rounded withers can make saddle fitting difficult. Secondly, and perhaps more important, the angle of the shoulder is related to the angle of the pastern, in that

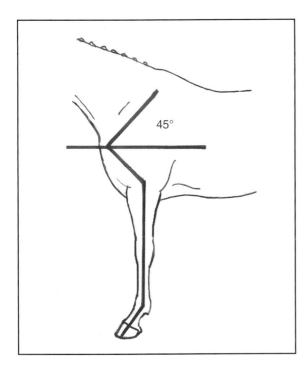

Fig. 1.7 Shoulder angles.

equality of the angle of these lines is indicative of symmetry and balance, and also dictates the way the horse moves. Thus a straight or upright shoulder often produces a shorter stride and therefore a somewhat 'choppy' way of going. In contrast a sloping shoulder results in a swinging stride, which although comfortable to sit on, often lacks the range of movement needed for optimum athleticism and jumping skills in the performance horse.

The horse's conformation and his natural way of going mean that he carries most of his weight on his forehand. He has evolved to have a big, heavy head, a full set of teeth and a long neck in order to maximize grazing opportunities, and the shoulders must support a lot of this weight. In the Thoroughbred horse the shoulders are often lower than the hindquarters: his biomechanical structure is such that his neck is set low to the wither, and this helps him go faster. For the racehorse this is the perfect evolutional development, but it is not necessarily helpful in the athletic event horse because if his neck is set on low to his shoulder this may predispose him to working on the forehand and he is then often naturally heavy in the hand when ridden.

In the warmblood and the Irish Sport Horse, on the other hand, selective breeding has led to the development of a horse with a neck that is set on higher to the withers, resulting in a more elevated forehand and thereby lightening the weight distribution through the shoulder. However, if the neck is set on high then the horse may appear 'peacocky' in his flatwork. Neither conformational trait will tell you if the horse has a natural ability to jump.

In recognition of certain desirable conformational traits and their characteristics, many breeds have been crossed to produce the ideal sports horse. Thus the Thoroughbred contributes speed, endurance and agility, and the warmblood athletic movement and the quality of its paces. The ISH is renowned for its jumping ability and sensible temperament.

The Chest and Heart Room

The width of the horse, as viewed from the front, should be considered. The chest needs to allow plenty of heart room and is the starting point for the fore limbs to extend out of the shoulder girdle to the floor. When viewed from the front ideally a straight line could be drawn down from the shoulder, through the middle of the knee and then centrally through the cannon bone to the middle of the hoof.

The horse in Fig. 1.8 has a great width of chest, indicative of plenty of heart room, which is desirable for the endurance aspect of the event horse. The forelimbs can be judged to be straight if a vertical line can be dropped from the top of the limb and run straight to the ground through the middle of the knee, the cannon bone, the pastern and then finally the middle of the hoof. If all these sections are equally balanced then the horse is more likely to be able to bear his weight evenly through the joints, and is less likely to be predisposed to soundness issues.

The Back and Hindquarters

The back is the area from the withers through to the top of the tail, and is identified in three sections: from just in front of the withers through to the last rib is the thoracic section; from the last rib to the top of the horse's hindquarters (the fusion with the pelvis) is the lumbar section; and from the pelvis to the tail is the sacral section. When a horse is identified as being long or short in the back it is with reference to the area from just behind the saddle to the top of the pelvis (the lumbar region). In a mare a slightly longer back is considered acceptable as it is indicative of a greater internal capacity whereby potentially to carry a foal. A longer back will enable the horse to become more supple laterally, but he may have difficulty with collection and in transferring power to the hind leg. A short back tends to be stronger in structure but may be limiting to suppleness, and may predispose the horse to conditions such as kissing spines. The ideal conformation will allow both strength and suppleness.

The hindquarters are the power house for the horse; they have the main gluteal muscles and the hamstring muscle group (semitendinous, semimembranosis and quadriceps femoris) that are responsible for driving the horse forwards (as in the Thoroughbred racehorse) and transmitting the power to the hind leg when developing collection and jumping power (as in the warmblood and ISH).

Fig. 1.8   Good forelimb conformation.

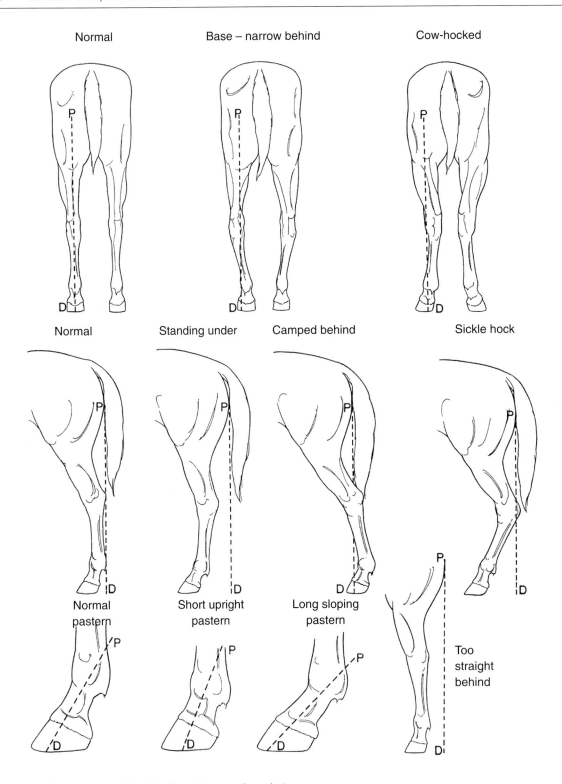

Fig 1.9   The anatomy of the hind leg (joints and angles).

The Hind Leg

The conformation of the hind leg is all about angles: from the pelvis to the hip, the hip to the stifle joint, the stifle joint to the hock, and finally the hock to the pastern. These joints allow greater or lesser flexion and consequently the transmission of power, resulting in the ability to collect for the increased power that is required in the dressage test at the higher levels, and for jumping and galloping. The hind leg should be under the horse: if the hock is out behind the quarters, this may predispose the horse to a weak back; if the angle formed by the hock is too straight then the flexion of the joints will be difficult (*see* Fig. 1.9).

When assessing the horse's movement, he should be able to swing the hind leg freely forward from the stifle. He should have a good overtrack in walk, since the extent by which he overtracks indicates his natural length of stride and relates directly to his galloping ability. However, too much overtrack can make it difficult for the horse to shorten through the hind leg and take more weight on to the hindquarters.

Viewed from behind, the same characteristics as in the forelimbs are desirable in the hind leg: thus to judge whether the limbs are straight it should be possible to draw a straight line from the point of the buttock through the hock and straight down to the ground through the centre of the heel. Some horses have slightly turned out hind feet, and a little rotation may be acceptable providing the hind limb conformation is fundamentally straight and correct; it is probably better if both hind feet turn out a little as this shows a balanced weight distribution, rather than one limb rotating more than the other.

The horse in Fig. 1.10 has a very symmetrical hind leg conformation. He is standing with his weight equally distributed through all his limbs, and the points of the buttocks, the hocks and fetlocks are level with each other. It is worth noting that the white socks on his pasterns are not equal, which draws the eye to the left foot due to the black colouring on the outside, making the limb appear to turn out from the fetlock down. Nevertheless the horse is very even in his weight distribution in that his hind legs are directly behind and in line with his forelimbs.

The horse in Fig. 1.11 has some weaknesses that run through to the hind limb. The most obvious is that she prefers to stand with her right hind turned out and away from the direct weight-bearing load of the limb: this is termed 'abduction'. As a result of this stance some muscle asymmetry has developed through from the gluteal and hamstrings. The horse will need a specific set of training exercises to make sure that this does not develop into a weakness when she is ridden and in training. However, she is only five years old, so age is on her side in correcting these imbalances.

The Lower Leg

The horse has no muscles below the knee and the hock, which means that the forearm and the second thigh provide the mechanical ability to move the lower limbs and stabilize the horse's balance. The skeletal structure is supported by ligaments and tendons, flexion and extension occurring by way of pulley and stay mechanisms. Many a serious injury occurs in the lower limb, largely because the blood supply to this area is limited, so good conformation is crucial in order to reduce the risk of injury and maintain soundness in the performance horse.

A performance horse should have a good amount of bone: this is measured according to the circumference of the top of the cannon bone just below the horse's knee. The amount of bone should be proportional to the height and build of the horse, although in the

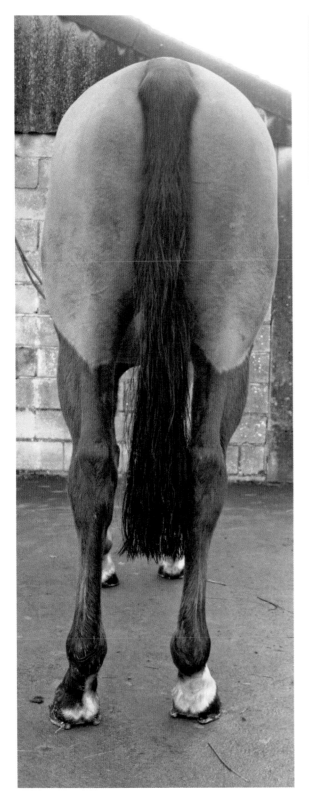

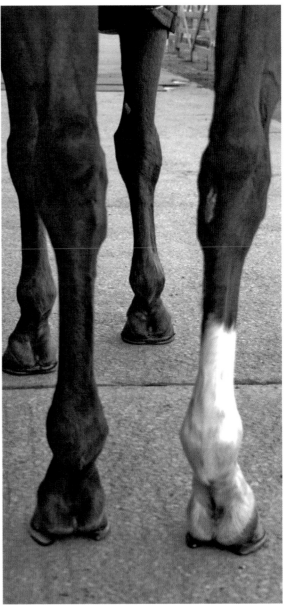

ABOVE: **Fig. 1.11   Weak hind leg conformation.**

LEFT: **Fig. 1.10   Good hind leg conformation.**

performance horse too much bone, whilst providing strength, can make him rather heavy and potentially slow.

Proportionally the forearm should be greater in length than the cannon bone: this is indicative of a compact and strong lower limb. It is essential that the cannon bone is set on straight to the knee. The tendons and ligaments mainly run from the back of the knee down behind the cannon bone and into the foot, and are secured by the annular ligament that runs round the fetlock joint. Ideally a tight appearance of these soft tissues is preferred, fleshy limbs being a sign of more common blood and, although they may have strength, they may also be rather heavy.

Poor conformational traits in the lower leg are 'back at the knee' and 'tied in' below the knee. 'Back at the knee' is where the

knee appears to be behind the vertical line from the shoulder through to the ground and is a most undesirable trait because the loading capacity of the limb is compromised when the horse has to gallop and jump. 'Tied in' below the knee is where the soft tissues – the deep digital flexor tendon, the superficial flexor tendon, the check ligament and the suspensory ligament – appear to be restricted just below the knee joint.

The Hoof

The hoof is hugely important to the soundness and performance of the athletic horse – hence the adage 'No foot, no horse'. The shape and structure of the hoof is often closely related to breed type; thus Thoroughbreds are noted for their poor foot conformation, often having a small flat hoof with a shallow heel and poor horn quality. The warmblood horse often has a more upright hoof, with plenty of heel but often with a restricted hoof/pastern angle (remembering that this angle is the same as that of the shoulder, and dictates how the horse moves). The ISH generally has good feet, a positive conformational trait for this breed.

The line that runs through the hoof-pastern axis in the forelimb should correspond to the shoulder angle, and ideally should form an angle of about 45–50° with the ground, although most importantly this should be equal to the shoulder axis. In the hind limb this angle should be about 50–55° (*see* Fig. 1.12). Sometimes the line of the hoof/pastern axis is not straight – known as 'broken' – due either to the straightness of the pastern or to the angle of the hoof wall. Such a broken line is a poor conformational trait as it reduces the load-bearing capacity of the limb and is a potential weakness that might affect the horse's soundness.

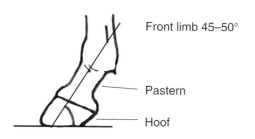

Front limb 45–50°

Pastern

Hoof

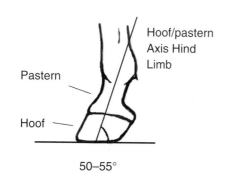

Pastern

Hoof

Hoof/pastern Axis Hind Limb

50–55°

Fig. 1.12 The hoof/pastern axis

BUYER BEWARE!

There are certain conformational defects and some injuries that the prospective buyer would be wise to avoid. Soft tissue damage such as tendon problems should be avoided. Even though modern veterinary procedures allow many horses to return to a good level of work, buying a horse with such an injury, without a full history of the cause, treatments and rehabilitation process, is potentially laying yourself open to future problems.

On the other hand, a few superficial lumps and bumps should not limit a horse's competitive career. Horses can be very accident prone and can knock themselves from an early age. I would, however, be concerned if a horse appeared to be especially accident prone, as this might indicate that he had poor natural balance in his way of going, and a general lack of coordination when in his natural environment. Acquired marks may not prevent a horse from being able to compete successfully to a certain level, though it is certainly preferable that a horse has no acquired lumps and bumps.

A concern with some lumps is their size and location; a splint, for example, would not want to be too large or risk articulating with the knee, and similarly a curb should be carefully assessed if it is big and in close articulation with the hock. The possible reason for their formation should also be considered.

Windgalls – a soft swelling behind the fetlock joint – may be just a sign of wear and tear, and many older horses will have some evidence of these. Caution would need to be taken if the horse only had one on one of his limbs, as this might indicate poor balance and limb loading. Windgalls are more commonly noted on the hind leg; on the front limbs they are generally more problematic.

ASSESSING THE HORSE IN MOVEMENT

A basic assessment of the horse's conformation is made when he is standing still; however, some traits only come to light when he is moving. It is always a good idea to see how a horse moves in his natural (i.e. not ridden). To assess conformation and the horse's balance and straightness he should be observed in walk and trot in a straight line: this will demonstrate the straightness of the flight of his limbs, and whether he dishes, plaits or turns one limb out more than another. Most important is that ideally he should do the same with both front legs and both hind legs in equal measure. Thus he should load each limb equally: if you close your eyes and listen to the horse walking or trotting, the sound of his feet striking the ground should be rhythmical. If one limb sounds louder than the other then the horse is loading that leg more, and hence is not carrying itself in balance. The horse should also load his feet evenly: as each foot makes contact with the ground, the loading of the foot surface should be equal. This can also be assessed by picking up the foot and looking at the wear pattern on the horse's shoe.

The Ridden Horse

The horse should move correctly in each of the three gaits: that is, he should be clear in the rhythm that he is working in. His ordinary medium walk should be naturally purposeful and cover the ground with an obvious overtrack. The working trot should give you the feeling of power and energy. It does not need to be extravagant as this can be difficult to contain and collect, but the trot should have some natural expression to it in order to produce a good dressage test.

Fig. 1.13   Correct medium walk.

The walk is a pace of relaxation, so we want to see the horse stepping freely forwards whilst seeking the contact. In Fig. 1.13 the horse is showing a good length of stride through the hind legs and the left fore is about to leave the ground and step forwards. The rider is fairly straight, but could be allowing a little more

through her elbows to improve the contact and allow the horse to stay connected.

The working trot should show a regular two-time rhythm with the horse showing expression in the stride as he leaves the ground. In Fig. 1.14 the horse is moving freely forwards and is seeking the contact well. The steps are free and

ABOVE: **Fig. 1.14   Correct working trot.**

BELOW: **Fig. 1.15   Correct working canter.**

the horse is about to step into the footprints left by the inside fore leg and so is tracking up correctly. The rider is riding forwards but has lost a little positional stability and has collapsed forwards looking down at the horse's head and neck; this is a very common rider error.

The canter is a pace of three time. In Fig 1.15 the horse is working forwards in a lovely uphill manner, taking the contact forward with the nose just in front of the vertical. The rider is sitting well and is looking ahead around the corner.

In the canter the horse should feel energetic and have a spring in his step. There should be a clear three-beat tempo to the canter: horses that tend to go in four time can be quite hard to improve, and this action may limit the horse's ability to cover the ground, which is necessary for all of the phases in eventing.

THE HORSE JUMPING

There are five phases to the horse's jump:

the approach, the take-off, the flight, the landing, and lastly the ride-away. These are terms that people use to analyse what the horse is doing. From a very basic perspective, the horse jumps by looking at what is in front of him, adjusts his balance to negotiate the obstacle and then jumps appropriately to avoid touching the fence. Some horses have this technique more naturally than others, but most horses can be trained to jump with some degree of confidence to a certain height and ability. The skill when assessing the horse's potential is to know where this level is in order to compete safely and within the comfort zone of the horse's physical ability.

In Fig. 1.17 the horse is jumping an upright set at about 1.10m. Most horses will not start to 'throw a shape' or make a correct 'bascule' until they have to jump a fence that is higher than their own elbows: only at this height does the horse have to engage his body and lift up through his abdomen and back. Here the horse is

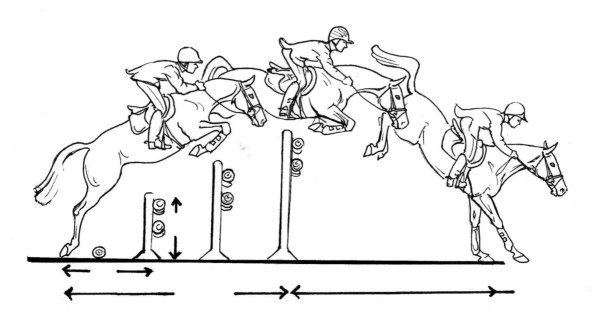

Fig. 1.16   Sequence of the bascule.

Fig. 1.17
This horse is
demonstrating
a correct
jumping
technique.

looking symmetrical in his frame over the
fence: he has approached the fence (first
phase of the bascule), taken off (second
phase) and is over the highest point of
the fence (third phase). This young horse
is naturally talented over a fence and is
making this fence appear easy. As he reaches
the highest point of the fence he will start
to lower his head, neck and forelimbs,
preparing for the fourth phase of the bascule
(the landing), and then the ride-away (last
phase).

He should naturally want to lift up through
his forearm and tuck up his front legs neatly
and evenly; he should jump with a rounded
back making a good shape with his hind legs,

TEMPERAMENT

Temperament should never be overlooked when considering the ideal event horse, and preference should be given to a horse with a little less ability but which will try his heart out for you and be consistent in his way of going. A talented horse with attitude can be very frustrating if he never really commits to the job and doesn't try for his rider. An honest, genuine horse will also be easier to fit in around a busy work schedule and the lifestyle that many working riders have.

which should leave the ground as a pair and follow the arc made by his body over the fence. On landing he should be light on his feet and move away in balance, being able to re-establish the canter naturally and without undue effort.

To summarize, whilst it is as important to assess the individual body segments for the ideal conformation, it is the overall impression that the horse gives to you that is critical. It is crucial that the proportions of his body and the way he carries himself are good if he is to stay fit, healthy and sound in a performance environment.

2 Fitness and Preparation

The aim when going eventing is to have a successful day, ideally completing on a double clear within the time, and finishing with a sound and happy horse and rider. It is the rider's responsibility to produce a horse that is fit for purpose, confident and skilled in the tasks that are to be set. It is also the rider's responsibility to be in control of their own health and fitness, and to address these needs throughout the whole year.

BASIC FITNESS PREPARATION FOR THE HORSE

The horse's fitness is not just about being able to ride him: the rider is responsible for his overall health and wellbeing, and should be aiming to produce 'a happy athlete', an objective endorsed by many of the disciplines, and something we need to address on a regular basis. For example, we need to ensure that he has his vaccination boosters: flu annually, and every six months for an FEI passport, and tetanus every two years – these are best given out of the competition season in case of adverse reactions. His teeth should be checked at least once a year by a BAEDT (British Association of Equine Dental Technicians) dental technician or vet.

Other aspects of care include his shoeing regime: ideally he needs attention from the farrier every six weeks, although this will depend upon the individual horse and the type of work he is doing. It is a good idea to carry a spare set of shoes in the lorry/trailer – maybe a used set which hasn't had too much wear: these can be used as replacements should he lose a shoe at a competition, and since they are his own shoes you know they will fit.

HEALTH CHECKS FOR THE HORSE

Health check	
Passport	Annual vaccinations
	Every six months if competing under FEI rules
Teeth	Annual attention by a vet or BAEDT dental technician
Shoeing	Approximately every six weeks
Worming	Every twelve weeks depending upon the faecal worm count; different wormers should be used throughout the year to target specific worms
Clipping	Throughout the winter months; the type of clip will depend upon the horse's workload and management regime
Weight	Monitor condition through the seasons

His general health and welfare also need to be addressed. Through the winter he will probably require some form of clip so that he can work without sweating unduly and will dry off quickly after exercise. Also his weight can fluctuate during the course of the season and should therefore be monitored, and his nutrition worked out accordingly throughout the year.

It is important to consider the fitness of the horse in order that he will be able to compete safely and comfortably without undue stress and strain on his body and mind. He needs to be fit for purpose, and this should be reflected in the training undertaken at home. A horse that is fit and well trained will be able to meet the demands of the competition easily and perform to the best of his ability. All too often a rider perceives the effort of the class as relating to the height that the horse has to jump and little else. At the lower levels the technical demands may not be very great but the physical effort does relate to the standard of the competition and should be taken seriously.

A good basic level of fitness for your horse will enable him to perform to his best and keep him happy and healthy. This will allow him to compete in the three activities, requiring control and relaxation in the dressage, calmness and obedience for the show-jumping, and finally stamina and bravery for the cross-country phase. If your horse has had a period of rest and been off work he may need bringing back into work slowly. To begin with he will need to spend some time – usually a minimum of six weeks – developing his musculoskeletal strength, hacking out in walk and trot on firm and consistent going such as roads and tracks. This is often referred to as 'slow work' and should not be neglected as it conditions the legs, tendons and ligaments and mildly stresses the skeleton (bones). This most basic of work should be carried out in his general hacking and relaxing days (non-schooling sessions). This type of work will of course vary according to the geography of the area, the availability of suitable hacking, and the behaviour of the horse. Because of the volume of traffic, roads nowadays are not always safe or pleasant to ride on, but we do need to establish a forward-thinking happy horse, and the best way to do this is by hacking across a variety of terrain.

Canter Work

Once a basic fitness has been developed, schooling work in an arena can begin along with some canter work and gymnastic jumping. The faster work should be developed gradually, up to a couple of times per week in a field or on a gallop, the canter sessions progressively increasing: this is known as 'interval training'. The horse needs to be fit enough to be able to do cross-country, meeting the demands of the course without unduly stressing himself. The majority of the horse's cross-country fitness work should be carried out in canter, although a base fitness in walk and trot is important to establish his musculoskeletal strength.

In the lower-level classes the horse should be able to complete the cross-country phase in a positive forward canter without the need to gallop, but the fitness work should still include cantering and galloping. The most important aspect of riding the course is to be able to maintain a rhythm that allows the horse to jump and canter confidently over a variety of terrain. It is important that the rider works the horse outside on grass to feel comfortable and confident in his ability to ride in a balanced position at a suitable speed. This can be achieved by establishing a known distance in a field or gallops and then timing how long it takes to cover this distance whilst maintaining the canter speed (see table on page 31).

HACKING OUT

This horse is looking relaxed and is quietly hacking out on a country lane. When possible it is important to take the horse out hacking on his own so that he develops self-confidence in where he is going and trust in the rider. Whenever hacking out, whether alone or in company, the yard should know where you are going and approximately how long you will be out for. This is a sensible approach to allow others to get help if you are having problems and have not returned to the stables when you are expected.

Fig. 2.1   Hacking out.

BRITISH EVENTING CROSS-COUNTRY SPEEDS (BE 2011)

Class	BE80	BE90/ BE90 Open	BE100/ BE100 Open BE100 Plus / BE100 JR	Novice/ ON/IN/ JRN/PT	Int/AI/OI	Advanced
Length	1600–2800	1600–2800	1600–2800	1600–2800	2400–3620	3250–4000
Speed in metres per minutes	435	450	475	520	550	570
Number of jumping efforts	18–25	18–25	18–25	18–28	22–32	25–40

Cross-country schooling, pleasure rides, hunting and hunter trials are all valuable ways to develop the event horse's fitness prior to competing. These activities educate the horse in travelling and behaving on the lorry, and in waiting and standing around at an event, they generally help to keep him mentally relaxed, and they allow both you and him to become familiar with working in different weather and ground conditions. Jumping smaller cross-country fences when out hacking, on a pleasure ride or at a hunter trial can support the fitness and education of you and your horse. It is also important that you have schooled over all types of cross-country fence – ditches, drops, banks and water – as well as negotiating a variety of conditions demanded by the terrain.

A rider should know how fast their horse covers the ground in order to work out the speeds required when competing. A simple way to do this is to set out an area in a field or on a gallop that is of a known distance, ideally about 200–400m long. By a simple calculation the rider can then work out the speed at which the horse should be covering the ground. For example:

Formula: $\dfrac{\text{distance in metres}}{\text{class speed in m. per min}} = \times\ 60\text{sec} = \text{time taken}$

For BE90 class $\dfrac{200\text{m}}{\text{BE90: }450\text{mpm}} = 0.44 \times 60 = 27\text{sec to cover }200\text{m}$

For training $\dfrac{200\text{m}}{500\text{mpm}} = 0.40 \times 60 = 24\text{sec to cover }200\text{m}$

When training we should canter at a slightly faster speed than is required in competition. This allows for the rider to be able to take a check, or to canter more slowly across uneven ground or changes in the gradient. A rider should be able to 'feel' the quality of the canter and be able to maintain a consistent rhythm whilst on the cross-country course. Watches are not permitted below Novice level when competing, the theory being that the rider should be able to ride in a balanced and consistent manner whilst jumping; however, to do this well requires some practice.

TACK AND EQUIPMENT

As eventing is a discipline that covers three specific phases, there is a certain amount of specialist tack and equipment that should be used for both safety and professional reasons. However, a word of warning: equestrian sports can be very trendy, and a lot of equipment is sponsored by professionals, but this does not mean that everyone needs to buy all the latest pieces of tack. Most important is that the tack is safe, that it fits the horse, and that it is being used appropriately.

Fig. 2.2 Horse and rider suitably turned out for working on the flat.

It is also a mistake to use new equipment at an event, even though it may be of the latest and safest design. Any new tack should be thoroughly worked in and used at home first so that you can be sure that it fits, and that it has had time to become soft and pliable: new leather can be rather stiff and can rub the horse if he is not accustomed to its fit. The same applies for the rider. If you have a new show jacket, jodphurs or boots, then these should be worn at home enough times to feel comfortable before they are put away for special use!

The Dressage Phase

In Fig. 2.2 horse and rider are suitably turned out for working on the flat. The horse is wearing a correctly fitted snaffle bridle and a dressage saddle – a saddle with a long flap allowing the rider to sit more centrally in the saddle whilst maintaining a close contact with the horse's sides through their leg position. The horse is wearing polo wraps that offer some protection and support to the legs when he is being ridden. Bandages and boots are not permitted for the dressage phase in the actual

Stud Type	Use
Road Stud	Often made of tungsten (very hard-wearing metal) on the tip of the nail that is driven into the shoe. These supply some additional grip when the horse is working on the roads; this is of particular benefit in the winter when the road conditions can be variable.
Spikes/Pointed Studs	These can be of various lengths, but in principle have a triangular point to them, often with a tungsten tip. The stud itself can be made of metal or synthetic material (available in different colours). They could be used when the ground is hard or slippery from recent rain/dew. Select the size that is appropriate to your horse's build and type.
Blunt/Square-ended Studs	As the name suggests, these are square-looking. The spikes can be of variable length. These are best used when the ground is wet and muddy, providing additional support on the turns. If the ground is excessively poor then it may be better not to use any studs as the ground will cut up under the hoof and studs may hinder the release of the foot and potentially catch the horse.
Hexagonal Studs	These have a hexagonal shape to the base of the stud, which limits the likelihood of the horse catching itself on the inside. They are usually more suited to firmer ground, although I use them on the inside of the shoe and a square-ended stud on the outside in sticky conditions.
Stud Hole Protectors	These are flat-ended studs that can screw into the stud hole, enabling the hole not to become blocked with mud and dirt. They are useful to put in the shoes the day before, when you should 'tap' out the stud holes, checking that the screw is working and the hole clean and able to take the stud. This saves a considerable amount of time at the show, and it is good practice to assess the condition of the shoe and stud holes prior to the event.

competition and so would need to be removed before entering the arena. The rider is dressed in appropriate and safe working clothing.

In fact it is not necessary to have a dressage saddle when competing at the lower levels of eventing. Although a dressage saddle will support the rider in a better position, it is more important to have a good jumping saddle that allows you to jump safely in both the show-jumping and cross-country phases, even if you have to ride on the flat with a slightly shorter stirrup length than you would have in a dressage saddle.

Many horses will benefit from studs in all three phases, so this should not be overlooked. It is useful to discuss the location of the stud holes with your farrier as there are various opinions about using one or two studs in each shoe. My personal preference is for two stud holes and I would usually use both as it balances the foot; however, it has been suggested that this can create torque on the limb and hence some people advocate one stud fitted on the outside edge of the shoe. Different studs may be needed for each phase due to changes in the ground conditions prevalent in each test.

Fig. 2.3   *Protective leather tendon boots.*

The Show-Jumping Phase

You may have to change your bridle for the show-jumping phase. If your horse needs a different bit for any of the phases then it is often safer, quicker and less stressful to have a separate bridle made up as required for each phase as there is often not enough time between phases to start swapping bits or nosebands. The horse may also require suitable boots, a martingale or breastplate.

Studs should be fitted, or checked and changed if necessary if they have been used in the dressage test but are not suitable for jumping. My personal preference is for two studs in each foot, as this balances the foot. The choice of stud will depend upon the ground, and the way the individual horse moves. Studs may be put in just the hind feet, or all round (front and back); again this will be according to the needs of the individual. It is advisable to school the horse at home on grass in all phases with studs in so he is secure and confident about wearing them: they should not be used for the first time in competition.

The Cross-Country Phase

As for the show-jumping, the rider will need to make sure that the horse is wearing a suitable bridle, breastplate and/or martingale

TOP: Fɪɢ. *2.4   Checking the studs in the front shoe before the cross-country.*

BELOW: Fig. *2.5   Cross-country boots taped over with coloured plastic tape.*

for the cross-country. Some form of protection should be worn on all the horse's legs, and the tack checked to make sure it is secure and will not slip, rub or move. This is particularly important if the horse gets hot and sweaty, or if the weather changes and conditions become wet and muddy. The studs should be checked to make sure they are secure and appropriate.

Many competitors tape their cross-country boots with coloured plastic tape for extra security and because it adds colour to their cross-country kit and co-ordinates with their body protector or jumper. The disadvantage of tape is that when the horse goes through water or mud, the boots tend to stretch and so does the tape, but when the boots return to their shape the tape does not, and as a result becomes loose, and can then slip and restrict the horse's movement. More solid leather boots may be preferable for the cross-country, as these tend to give the horse more protection and support than neoprene boots. There is, however, a whole range of strong and durable lightweight synthetic boots available for the cross-country if leather is not your preference. Many modern boots have double strapping, thereby reducing the need for additional taping.

The rider should wear a suitably fitted body protector, a hat of correct and safe specification (every hat must be checked and tagged by the event secretary on the first occasion of competing with it), a medical card on their arm, and non-slip gloves (*see* Fig. 2.4).

CROSS-COUNTRY SCHOOLING

When going schooling it is good practice to take a trainer with you. This person should be knowledgeable about the level that you and your horse are working at, and be aware of your competition aims for the season. It is advisable to go in a group, as a lead can be offered for a nervous horse or rider if required, and it is generally safer.

Fig. 2.6   When going schooling it is advisable to take a trainer with you.

BASIC FITNESS PREPARATION FOR THE RIDER

Modern lifestyles have changed much of how we work and live. Everything nowadays happens at rapid speed, and we are expected to fit our work, family and leisure pursuits into a twenty-four-hour period simply by being better organized and more efficient in our time management. The down side of these expectations is that we drive more frequently than we walk, we utilize the internet for shopping and information rather than going to a retail outlet, our relaxation is often based around the television and the internet, and we can purchase convenience foods that are quicker to prepare and to eat. All of these modern lifestyle influences have made us less fit as a nation than we were a decade ago. One consequence of this is that, whilst the horse provides an element of relaxation and exercise for the rider, there is often a lack of rider fitness in the athletic sense.

Most riders will have a base level of fitness from general stable duties, work around the yard and riding their horse. However, unless this is the rider's primary job it is unlikely to be sufficient to make them fit enough to compete. A rider who only has one or two horses will probably need to do more than just ride in order to maintain a fitness level that is sufficient to support their horse when they are competing: by being fitter they are in a better position to support the horse if he gets himself into trouble as a result of fatigue or because he is distracted, which is more likely to occur in the latter part of the cross-country course. If the rider is unfit they can potentially lose balance and therefore postural independence, and may hamper the horse's ability to perform, resulting in faults at the fences and perhaps even a fall.

In preparing for the eventing season, the rider should address their nutrition and hydration status. Too often we plan how to feed our horses but neglect ourselves. Looking after our diet should be an important part of our preparation for the new season, and not something to consider the day before when we pack the lorry. Our horses frequently have to fit in around our busy work schedule, so we should make sure that we are in a fit and healthy state to function effectively.

Cross Training

When we have only our own horse to look after alongside a full-time job, then riding as the only form of exercise is probably not sufficient to support the fitness level that is required if we intend to event competitively. The human body has a strong ability to adapt to exercise, and one of the best ways to do this is to challenge it by cross training or mixing different types of exercise. Cross training allows the body to incorporate the use of other muscles to keep the body balanced, so that a balanced muscle structure can be developed: this in itself leads to a reduced risk of injury and helps avoid certain muscles getting tight and others weak through lack of use. Riders often suffer from a general overuse of the shoulders and poor core (pelvic) stability. Consequently these areas may be predisposed to injury on a day-to-day basis or through trauma caused by falling off. Knowing that such specific riding injuries are likely, it would be prudent for riders to condition themselves into developing their physical fitness levels so as to reduce the impact on the whole body and in particular these injury sites.

Cardiovascular Fitness

People come in all sorts of different shapes and sizes with different work/life commitments. Looking after a horse in DIY livery will help to support some muscle groups just by the physical nature of mucking out, lifting haynets and walking to turn out and fetch the horses in. However, although this type of general work builds up a basic muscular skeletal fitness, it does not address our cardiovascular needs or our balance and postural development. Cardiovascular fitness is addressed through aerobic exercise, which in turn helps to increase our concentration and reaction times: these are relevant if we want to develop quicker response and reaction times when riding and specifically competing. Aerobic exercise will also support our general riding, and in particular periods of endurance work such as hunting, pleasure rides and long competitive days. Strength and coordination training is also needed to support rider posture and balance; this type of exercise is recognized through Pilates, yoga and basic gym work, and aims to balance the muscles utilized for riding and postural control.

Fig. 2.7 Running is an activity that can be carried out almost anywhere at anytime. Do make sure you have comfortable clothing and, most importantly, suitable footwear.

PROFESSIONAL ADVICE

Whatever the type of exercise you undertake, it is advisable to seek professional advice and support from a fitness professional to correct your posture and ensure the maximum gain from your choice of exercise. These trainers can support your needs by putting a specific training programme together. You should use the same criteria that you would for selecting your riding trainer: high on the list should be personal recommendation, and working with a trainer who understands the specific demands of competitive riding.

Types of Exercise

A rider will only pursue another method of exercise if they like it, so it is important to find one they enjoy and which they can maintain. They need to establish a basic level of cardiovascular fitness, so anything to raise the heart rate for thirty minutes, four or five times per week will increase a person's fitness. Such activities could include swimming, running/jogging, cycling and gym work.

Swimming is a non-impact activity, so is ideal if a rider has joint problems, is overweight or is new to fitness training. It is excellent for developing core strength and for body toning, and swimming lengths provides a good source of aerobic training. Swimming is a good activity for the winter months and dark cold nights, and can be very sociable if a few friends get together and arrange to meet and swim on a regular basis.

Running or jogging has a higher impact on the body and joints, so is not ideal for some people with certain injuries. Nevertheless it is excellent for developing

ANNUAL TRAINING CYCLE FOR THE RIDER

Month	Activity
January	Winter conditioning (looking after the horse), possible limited riding opportunities Fitness: cardiovascular 3–4 × weekly, swim, gym session, cycle (spin class), run
February	Winter conditioning (looking after the horse), possible limited riding opportunities. Compete where possible in dressage and show-jumping Fitness: cardiovascular 3–4 × weekly, swim, gym session, cycle (spin class), run Organize diary when eventing schedule is published
March	Clocks change at end of month, giving the opportunity to ride in the evenings. Increase riding and schooling as ground, weather and time permit. Start riding shorter to support fitness levels in canter work and cross-country schooling
April	Competing
May	Competing
June	Competing
July	Competing, consider holiday and family commitments
August	Competing, consider holiday and family commitments
September	Competing
October	Competing
November	Reflect on your own performance over the season, re-evaluate goals, targets on personal level Evaluate your personal fitness, your energy levels and any acquired injuries Establish a fitness programme for yourself over the winter: cardiovascular 3–4 × weekly, swim, gym session, cycle (spin class), run Plan the horse's needs, too, for the winter months: time off, and work schedule to return to work for the following season
December	Manage work, horse and family commitments around Christmas and the holiday period Fitness: cardiovascular 3–4 × weekly, swim, gym session, cycle (spin class), run

musculoskeletal and cardiovascular fitness. Many running clubs welcome anyone from complete beginners to serious runners, and this is often more fun than trying to commit to running on your own or on a treadmill in a gym.

Cycling is great aerobic exercise as well as a means to developing good balance and coordination skills, both of which are relevant to riding. It may be possible simply to start cycling to the yard when the weather permits, or at weekends when there is generally more time. Another way to enjoy this activity is to attend spinning classes at a local gym.

Pilates and yoga are both great for developing balance, flexibility and core strength, all of which are essential for horse riders, and which will help maximize their stability and develop an independent position when riding. There are now classes for Pilates on horseback, which is a fun way to combine both activities.

Rider Fitness Exercises

Exercise One: The Plank

The plank is a simple and easy way to work the core (pelvic) stability of the rider; it is also relatively easy to do correctly on your own. Some other exercises are best initially taught and trained with the support of a gym instructor or personal trainer, as an exercise carried out incorrectly can be detrimental to posture and muscular stability, and may potentially cause injury.

The aim of this exercise is to stabilize the core abdominal and pelvic muscles, thus supporting the postural stability of the rider when riding. It is developed as follows:

- First a suitable place must be found to carry out the exercise: preferably the rider should have a mat to lie on, thereby reducing the strain through the shoulders and pressure on the elbows; this will be more comfortable than lying on a carpet or the floor.

- The rider should initially lie on the mat facing downwards, then they should raise themselves on to their toes (the exercise can be performed in bare feet or trainers). The weight is then taken on to the elbows, with the elbows bent at 90 degrees. The back should remain straight with the stomach pulled in to engage the core muscles around the pelvis and to stop the back from dropping.

- It is not uncommon for people to drop the hips, losing the straight line from the shoulders through the back to the toes; if this occurs then too much pressure can be placed on the lower back. It is better to encourage the hips to be higher initially than to use the back muscles excessively. If raising straight to the toes is difficult the weight can be placed just on to the knees until better strength and coordination is developed.

- This posture should be held initially for thirty seconds. A rest of a minute of two can be taken (or ideally this can be interspersed with other exercises), then the exercise repeated.

- The exercise can be developed gradually until the posture can be held for two minutes.

- Variations can be made, so that instead of lying prone the person rotates at 90 degrees so they are sideways to the ground, with the weight being taken on the side of the foot or shoe and on the lower arm. This posture can be held for thirty seconds. The exercise should then be performed on the other side to make sure that stability is developed equally on both sides.

Exercise 2: Cardiovascular work

Cardiovascular training is a simple way to develop greater lung capacity and riders will immediately feel the benefit when riding, galloping and generally working with the horses. It is integral to the fitness requirements for skilled cross-country riding.

The aim of the exercise is to improve the cardiovascular response through training adaptations, and it should be developed as follows:

- A basic assessment of the rider's fitness and health should be considered; a doctor's consent should be sought if there are any underlying medical conditions that limit/restrict the type of cardiovascular work to be undertaken.
- Before you start any exercise session make sure you have the correct equipment, such as trainers, underwear, safety helmet: this can make a huge difference to your performance and progress, and your feeling of competence and improvement.
- Whatever the type of training (running, swimming, cycling), a basic plan should be put in place to develop a suitable training programme over several months. Ideally set a route where both distance and terrain are comfortable, and which can be repeated if necessary. It is always more rewarding to have a circular route rather than one where you have to turn round and return. A field is quite suitable for running around, and good well lit roads for cycling are recommended. Swimming pools usually have specific times allocated to lane swimming, which is far less stressful than trying to swim against a crowd.
- Set a realistic time scale for repeating the programme. Ideally some form of cardiovascular work twice a week will stabilize a person's fitness, and three times a week will advance their fitness. Start slowly and gradually build up. Ten minutes of running followed by a three-minute rest for three repetitions is quite suitable to start with. If swimming, set a realistic number of lengths for your level of fitness, followed by a break, and repeat this cycle for thirty minutes. If cycling, find a route where you can go quickly enough for ten minutes to raise your heart rate, then rest for a few minutes, and repeat the cycle three times so your total cycling time is thirty minutes, as you did for the running cycle.
- After a week or two, depending upon how you feel and are progressing, you can increase the amount of time exercising, and this can be increased weekly until an hour is possible and can be maintained comfortably. If exercise time is limited, then the running and cycling can be carried out on hills, as this is more demanding than on level ground and so does not need to be carried out for so long.
- Once you are comfortable with an hour's exercise the rest periods can be reduced or the intensity of the work increased (speed and/or effort). Do make sure that you are using the best technique for the activity. If pain or discomfort is felt beyond the initial lack of fitness then expert advice and guidance should be sought from a doctor or sports professional.

PLANNING AHEAD

Many people fit in eventing around a regular job, and if this is the case for you, then it is important to consider the impact that it will have on your daily life. Planning ahead into the next season will allow you to fit in your eventing around work commitments and holiday times. Many British Eventing events run in the week, and this will need to be factored into your work leave entitlements. Weekend events can be heavily oversubscribed and entries can get balloted. Consider the events that you wish to compete in, how local they are, and if they run in the week. As soon as the event schedule is published, make a list of the events you want to compete at, those that you would like to go to and the distance to these venues.

Competing is not a cheap activity, so it is useful to work out a budget for the year. This should include how many BE events you wish to attend, entry fees, start fees, distance (fuel expenses) and any overnight stabling needs. Once you have a cost allocated to the actual competitions you will need to consider training costs. This may include going to shows run by other affiliated bodies, such as show-jumping with British Show Jumping (BSJ) and British Dressage (BD); both disciplines offer discounted membership in the form of either day tickets or half-year membership, both of which are ideal for training over the winter and spring. For more details *see* Further Information, page 164.

Once these costs have been assessed, then you can consider training/coaching support. British Eventing provides a list of BE accredited trainers/coaches who are fully up to date with the training needs of event riders from grass roots to advanced level. A list of trainers can be found on the BE website (see Further Information). Some riders like to use different trainers for each of the three phases; however, the advantage of using a specific eventing trainer is that they appreciate the skills needed by both horse and rider across each of the phases and also the relationship between the phases, so they are uniquely placed to support all aspects of training and competing for eventing. Throughout the winter months other organizations such as British Riding Clubs provide regular training sessions for their members: this can be a sociable way to meet like-minded riders, and enjoy a structured training session, often in an indoor school, therefore maintaining a training plan through the winter months.

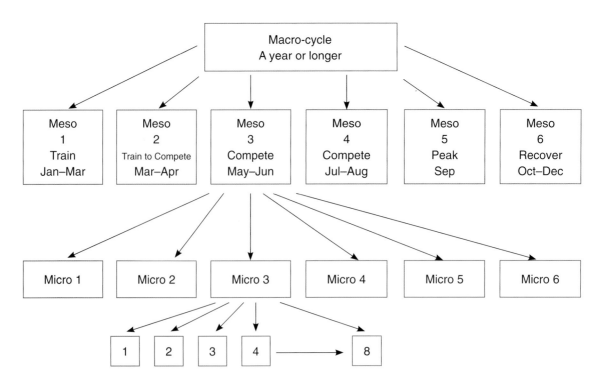

Fig. 2.8   Periodization overview.

ANNUAL TRAINING CYCLE FOR THE HORSE

Month	Activity
January	Begin to increase workload if horse has been resting, develop musculo-skeletal fitness, roadwork, hacking
	If in work continue with skill development through schooling, dressage, show-jump training and competitions. Maybe hunting
February	Continue with skill development through schooling, dressage, show-jump training and competitions; aim to be competing at or above the level to be aimed at within the event season. Maybe hunting
March	Increase cardiovascular work – cantering and cross-country schooling
April	Competing – period of competing, reflection and assessment of the goals set, may need to re-evaluate as season progresses
May	Competing
June	Competing
July	Competing
August	Competing, consider holiday periods, ground conditions
September	Competing, stepping up a level before ending the season
October	End of the event season. Review season, assessment of level and classes competed and success rate, consider performance in each phase, fitness and any acquired injuries
November	Rest period, opportunity to evaluate the season. Review long-term goals, set or adjust short-term goals for the next season. Reduce work load if allowing horse to have some time off
December	Time off or steady exercise. May be weather dependent with limited opportunity to ride except at weekends

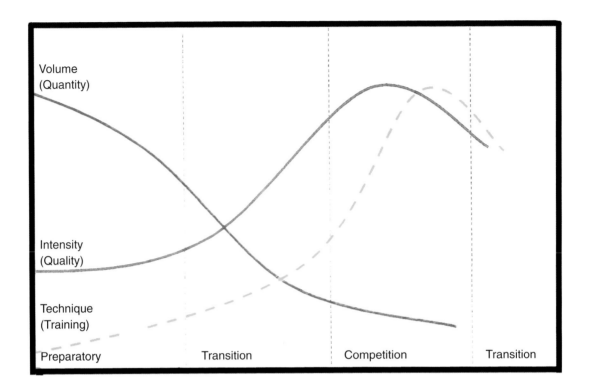

Fig. 2.9 Matveyev's model of periodization.

TRAINING PROGRAMME FOR HORSE AND RIDER

Periodization

The aim of training is to improve performance. The process of breaking down the training programme into manageable units, each with its own goal, is known as periodization. Many strength, conditioning and fittening programmes can effectively improve human and equine performance, but knowing how to utilize the programme is the key to success. In the early days of sports training, pre-season, competition and recovery phases were enough, but as knowledge, technology and methods have advanced, training has become much more sophisticated. The 'system' of periodization was established for athletes to prevent 'overtraining' and to optimize peak performance through training cycles. A main goal is to establish progressive sport-specific training that promotes peak performance and reduces the risk of injury.

Periodization Cycle

Macrocycle:
● Overall training period (for example one year, four years).
● Annual championship or Olympics.

Mesocycle:
● Within the macrocycle are several mesocycles, which can be weeks to months depending on programme goals and the rider's fitness levels and aims.

- Mesocycles must be systematic in their design.
- Meso 1 – general fitness work: this stage is known as 'training to train'.
- Meso 2 – more specific speed/strength work: intensity of training increases considerably.
- Meso 3 – start of the competitive season, general training is reduced and replaced by competitive work. Qualifying for a championship.
- Meso 4 – training is reduced to avoid over-use and to allow the body to recover.
- Meso 5 – 'peaking': the culmination of competition.
- Meso 6 – the recovery phase, during which the body is allowed to recover from a vigorous season.

Microcycle:
- Within each mesocycle are a number of microcycles, which include periods of seven training days.

Matveyev's Model

Matveyev's model can be applied to both the horse and the rider. In the preparatory phase there is a high volume of fitness training for the rider: this is most likely to take place between January and March. It can take the form of stable and yard duties which will have some endurance aspects to training, but more specifically an additional form of cardiovascular training such as swimming, running or cycling should be considered. For the horse, this is a period of fittening and cardiovascular training too, taking the form of hacking, cantering and developing the faster work. The intensity of the workload will increase for both horse and rider as the weather changes from winter through to the spring. The technical training will also start to increase for both parties; this will take the form of flatwork and dressage schooling, gymnastic jumping and some training competitions that are within the comfort zone for both horse and rider.

The transitional phase will be as the season changes into spring and the competition season draws closer. The volume of cardiovascular training may decrease, but the intensity will increase; this translates as improving the fitness of the rider and developing more fast work for the horse (less slow work and the introduction of faster work). The training regime will increase to meet the demands of the competitions that are being aimed at in the forthcoming year, hence it is important to link this to the goals set by the rider.

During the competition phase the workload volume will probably decrease as both horse and rider will have rest periods after competitions, and the events themselves will stimulate the cardiovascular and respiratory fitness of both horse and rider. The intensity of the training will be geared to meet the demands of each competition, with reflection between events as to what needs improving, as will the skill training which is reflected through the technical aspects of the competitions. This period will have a wave effect, the curve indicating the individual's competitions over the season, with each peak being an event and the trough between being the rest and recovery period, before building up to the next event.

The transitional phase is a period of reflection on the season's performance, the opportunity to recover from any physical injuries and aches and pains. This is the optimum time for the rider to address positional imbalances from falls and postural changes in their body. For the horse, similar considerations should be given alongside some rest time before re-establishing the training programme for the next year. For both parties this time should link into the aims and objectives for the following season, and be built into future aims and goal planning.

3 Dressage Training

There are various levels of dressage test in the eventing structure, all of which are similar in standard to the tests prescribed by the affiliated body British Dressage for the different levels at their competitions. By understanding the levels and requirements of the British Dressage tests, the rider can develop and train the horse to meet the standards that are required in eventing. At a fundamental level the horse initially needs to be working along similar lines to BD Preliminary and Novice standards.

The dressage aspect of the horse's training

Fig. 3.1 A good working trot, the horse looking happy and healthy. However, she is really only fit for initial schooling work, being unclipped and rather too fat.

should be developed out of the competition season, as this allows time for the horse to work out any new movements and to develop the physical and mental acceptance of the demands that are being made on his mind as well as his body. This work will also help develop his fitness and prepare him for the demands of competition when the season begins. In comparing the horses in Figs 3.1 and 3.2 it is evident that in Fig. 3.1 the mare is fit for schooling but is somewhat out of condition, as she is carrying rather too much weight, and she is not clipped: this is acceptable for the initial stages of

Fig. 3.2 Fit to compete.

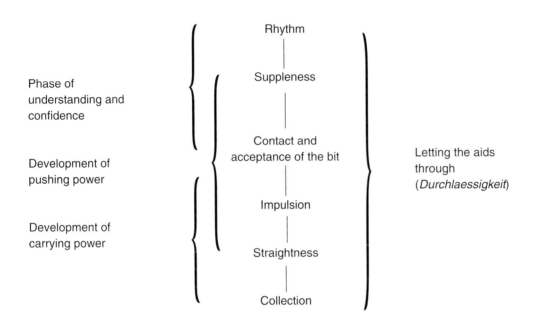

Fig. 3.3   The Scales of Training.

training, but once her cardiovascular work is stepped up she will need clipping to support the increased work and fitness level. In Fig. 3.2 the horse is ready to compete, being fitter and leaner, with a tighter abdominal structure and a good muscle tone to her neck, shoulders and quarters.

THE SCALES OF TRAINING

As well as appreciating what is required in the different levels of British Dressage test, a rider should understand the Scales of Training, which are structured to show the development of the horse based upon the German training system dating back to classical principles; these are now firmly embedded in the British philosophy of training the horse and should be incorporated into all levels of dressage and jump training. There are six sections that make up a complete cycle of education for the horse, and these are divided into three sub-sections. Whilst they should be looked at together, they do also need to be considered individually for each horse, relating it to his education and physical development.

Rhythm

The first Scale of Training. Rhythm is fundamental to the horse's way of going and very important. Each horse should have a clear rhythm for each of the three paces, and an appropriate tempo (speed of the rhythm) for each gait. Without rhythm the horse will struggle to develop a suitable balance at the most basic of levels. The rhythm in the horse's movement needs to be consistent both when working in straight lines and when turning and changing direction. The rhythm should be maintained through transitions from one pace to another, as well as within the pace.

Suppleness and Looseness

The second Scale of Training. This represents the horse's ability to develop suppleness in both a vertical (up and down) direction, and also laterally (left and right) in order to work softly and be loose and flexible through his whole body. For the horse to be truly supple, he needs to be free from tension, both physically and mentally, and must show the ability to work through his back, softly and with mobile joints, and to be attentive to his rider. If a horse is working correctly and happily he will have a relaxed demeanour to his expression, his ears will be relaxed and slightly turned out, his back should swing

rhythmically within the pace, and his tail should be soft and carried in time to the working gait.

Contact (Acceptance of the Bit)

The third Scale of Training. Contact refers to the connection that the rider has to the horse's mouth through the rein via his hand ('feel'). The horse should be going freely forward from the leg and then 'look' forward to take the rein forward and down, thus establishing the contact and connection through the rider's aids. A supportive contact will work in conjunction with the balance of the horse and be appropriate to the horse's stage of education and way of going. Contact is often difficult to establish in the younger or less educated horse. The rein pressure should always be

Fig. 3.4
Not on the contact.

taken forwards and never 'pulled' backwards, as this compromises the horse's ability to be ridden forwards from the rider's leg into the yielding hand, thus securing the connection and contact. Contact is achieved when the horse accepts the bit; however, the natural conformation of the horse's mouth needs to be considered when selecting a bit so that it is suitable for the individual horse.

Figs 3.4 and 3.5 show the difference between a horse that is not working to a contact, and one that is. It is very easy for a horse to lose concentration temporarily, particularly if young, as the five-year-old in Fig 3.4 is demonstrating. The important thing is that the rider is able to stay correct in their position, and still in their hand, in order to ride the horse forwards from the leg to re-establish the contact and the connection. If the horse is always allowed to work like this, then the incorrect muscles and way of going can become established. Lungeing may help the horse to be more confident in taking the rein forward.

In Fig. 3.5 the horse is happily taking the rein forward and seeking the contact. The horse's nose should be on, or just in front of, the vertical, with the poll at the highest point. Here, the rider has slightly tipped so that she is leaning on her hands, which may make the contact feel heavier than it needs to be. If she lifts her shoulders this should lighten the contact and help the horse work more to the hind leg.

Impulsion

The fourth Scale of Training. Impulsion is the energy that is created from the hind leg: power is transmitted through the movement of the hind legs to push the horse forwards. The horse should be energetic in how the hind legs are pushed off from the ground. When viewed from behind, the whole of the horse's foot should be seen as he pushes from the surface and takes

Fig. 3.5 On the bit, taking the contact forward.

the foot and limb in flight to the next step. When working in trot and canter there should be a spring to the horse's step, allowing the generated power to go forwards in a relaxed manner with an active hock action (flexion of the joint). The generated movement is absorbed through the horse's back, which should swing, allowing the rider to sit softly and absorb the movement.

Straightness

The fifth Scale of Training. Most animals are not born straight – including the human.

Straightness in the horse means the forehand or shoulders are in line with the hindquarters. Straightness also allows for the horse to have an equal distribution of weight through the body (within these two sections). If the horse is able to work in good balance and straight he will be biomechanically more efficient and less predisposed to injury and wear and tear. Most horses are naturally crooked, and this, combined with their anatomical structure (the horse's shoulders are narrower than his

ABOVE: *Fig. 3.6   Not straight.*

RIGHT: *FIG. 3.7   Straight.*

hindquarters) leads to a lack of straightness. When the horse has established a suitable balance and way of going to be straight, he will be more efficient at utilizing the energy in his hindquarters, thus working more equally.

In Figs 3.6 and 3.7 the first horse is not straight, and the second horse is. Thus in Fig. 3.6 the horse is working on the left rein but is clearly showing right bend through the neck. The rider has allowed herself to be pulled forward and so is unable to sit up straight and free up her shoulders and arms to be independent in her position. She needs to turn her shoulders slightly to the inside with an open inside rein to support the flexion in the direction of travel. She may also have an uneven stirrup length, which should be addressed once she is working in a straight line.

In Fig. 3.7 the horse is showing good straightness and is working freely forwards on the right rein. He is correct through his body, with his nose on the vertical and his poll at the highest point. The rider is sitting up vertically but is collapsing to the inside through her left hip and so is not straight herself.

Collection

The sixth and last Scale of Training. To be working in collection the horse must be able to carry his weight equally across all four limbs. He needs to be able to flex the joints in his hind leg (fetlock, hock, stifle and hip) to allow greater weight transfer, reducing the angle between these joints and then taking more weight on to the hind leg so as to lighten the shoulders. This weight transfer is achieved through the horse bending his hind legs more, allowing them to step further underneath him and taking shortened, more energetic, higher steps. The consequence of developing collection is to lighten the shoulders and forehand, increasing the mobility and freedom of the horse.

A horse can develop his training through all of the Scales of Training, but at the lower levels the first three are critical. Without a basically balanced horse that is confident in the first phase it is not possible to progress to the last phase in a secure and constructive manner. Completion of the horse's education in all of the Scales takes some time. He must be strong and fit enough to maintain his balance and coordination as he moves through his educational development. It is possible for the novice horse to be secure in the first three Scales in his basic way of going but then lose his rhythm when higher level work is introduced, such as lateral work. It is then imperative to return to the basic way of going to re-establish the rhythm, suppleness and contact before moving on. No shortcuts can be taken if the long-term athletic ability and soundness of the horse are to be safeguarded.

TACK AND EQUIPMENT

The Saddle

For the horse to perform comfortably the rider needs to be able to sit in balance and harmony with the horse. At the lower levels it is not imperative for the rider to have a dressage saddle, although it is desirable. What is important is that the saddle fits both the horse and rider. A jumping saddle is an important investment and may be the most suitable saddle to use (and certainly preferable to a General Purpose (GP) saddle). If you do ride your dressage test in a jumping saddle, remember that it is designed for the rider to be sitting predominantly out of the seat. With this in mind you will not be able to ride at a long stirrup length similar to a dressage saddle, but will need to find a suitable length that keeps you in balance when riding on the flat.

Fig. 3.8   The horse working correctly. She is freely moving, carrying her head on the vertical. She shows a relaxed and happy way of going while schooling in the field.

In Fig. 3.8 the rider is using a jumping saddle but is working on the flat. Her stirrup length is longer than it would be for jumping, but shorter than if she were riding in a dressage saddle. She shows a secure and independent position, riding in balance with the horse, which is working forwards to the contact.

The Bridle

The most important aspect of the bridle is the fit of the bit and the tension of the tack around the nose and poll. Various bridles are available that disperse the pressure around the horse's head through tack construction or design of the bridle. The snaffle bit should lie about 1–2cm

Fig. 3.9   A correctly fitted snaffle bridle.

Thoroughbreds have a more refined mouth with more room to move their tongue, but often have a narrow jaw and object to tight tack that causes pressure around the head. Horses that are sensitive in the mouth and very mobile or fussy may go better in a fixed eggbutt bit ring, which stabilizes the contact, whereas those that tend to be heavy in the hand may be better in a loose-ring bit, which limits the opportunity for the horse to fix on the hand.

The age of the horse also needs consideration. For instance, horses under five years are still forming their incisor teeth, and may have wolf teeth which can cause discomfort (and should be removed by your equine dentist). A flash noseband may aggravate the pressure on these already sensitive regions, so a drop noseband or a cavesson may be more suitable. Horses between six and eight years may still be experiencing molar development and may not like pressure across their jaw, so a grakle or a drop noseband may be advisable as these avoid pressure on these sensitive areas.

In Fig. 3.9 the snaffle bridle is fitted correctly, though ideally at a competition it would be better to remove the martingale stops for the dressage phase as they might distract from the overall impression that the horse gives when he is doing his test. The browband is correct around the ears and the head. The cavesson noseband is fitted so that it sits just under the projecting cheekbone, which allows the flash strap to be fitted firmly without pulling the cavesson down the nose. The horse is wearing a hanging cheek snaffle which is fitted rather low, but is appropriate for the mouth conformation of this horse.

Non-Permitted Equipment

In the British Eventing rule book there are clear and explicit rules regarding the tack, training aids and equipment that are permitted in competition. These are for the safety and

(½–1 in) wider than the mouth, and sit so that the corners of the mouth are not pulled up too high: one to two wrinkles on the lips is a good guideline for correct placement. In particular your horse's mouth should be assessed, as some breeds have a head conformation that impacts upon the space for the bit. For example warmbloods can have very fleshy lips and a thick tongue, and often a double-jointed snaffle with a slim mouthpiece can benefit this conformation type as it allows for more tongue room. Ponies are similar to warmbloods, and often have a relatively small mouth so do not appreciate a wide or chunky mouthpiece.

Fig. 3.10   Flatwork in a jumping saddle.

welfare of both horse and rider and should be referred to for current guidelines. When training and educating the horse there may be occasions when this prohibited equipment is suitable and acceptable to use. Sometimes an overly fresh or strong horse may school better in his jumping tack or with a martingale rather than in his dressage bridle. It may also be necessary for a horse to work in a hackamore or bitless bridle if he has a sore mouth or tooth issues. Whatever the reason for the choice of tack and equipment, the training and acceptance of the equipment (bits, martingales, training aids) should be paramount.

Training Surfaces

Modern-day culture is such that most yards have an artificial surface in a marked-out arena on which to work and school their horses. It means that we can work our horses all year round and at various times of the day so that we can fit them into our work/life balance. It is an excellent idea to be able to work your horse in a controlled area that is the same size as the dressage arena you compete in (20 x 40m or 20 x 60m). Being familiar with the letters and the dressage movements and their requirements is an excellent way to practise the demands of the test in competition. However, when competing at an event the horse will most likely be performing his test on grass, and will be working in on the same type of going, so it is good practice to make sure that some of your training is carried out in the field at home so you know how your horse will cope with the space and the change of the going. Inevitably ground conditions will also vary from one event to another, so both you and your horse must be confident about working in firm or muddy conditions.

STRUCTURING THE DRESSAGE TRAINING

A dressage test comprises a series of movements with a smaller series of collective observations at the end of the test, namely 'Paces', 'Impulsion', 'Submission' and finally 'Rider Position'. The judge awards marks out of ten for each of the movements, and then summarizes the horse's general way of going for the whole test within the collectives, again each marked out of ten. The 'Paces' are marked against the horse's ability to stay in rhythm through the regularity and freedom of the gaits seen. 'Impulsion' reflects the horse's desire to go forward, the elasticity of the steps, the suppleness of the back and the engagement of the hindquarters.

'Submission' is assessed according to the horse's attention and confidence in his performance, the harmony, lightness and ease of the movements, as well as the lightness of the forehand. Lastly the influence of the rider is considered through their ability to maintain a good position and seat as well as the correctness and effect of their aids.

All the marks are added up and then through a coefficient, a penalty mark is taken forward to the jumping phases. The collective comments are really critical in assessing the consistency of your performance at any level. Regardless of the specific test, the weather or your horse's mood, the collectives are a benchmark for your ability to produce the demands (related to the Scales of Training) and the directives of the test. Knowing how your performance is assessed allows you to develop the fundamental training plan for you and your horse to be successful, and achieve a low penalty mark.

It is important to understand the temperament of your horse: some are rather hot and quick in their reactions, whilst others are naturally slower and have a steadier outlook on life. However, whatever his temperament, it is important that you can work with the horse so that he is happy and confident to work with you. Horses do not need drilling, and an event horse has to be multi-skilled by the nature of the disciplines; however, flatwork will underpin all of his ridden training, and the canter work in particular will have a direct influence on his jumping ability.

Horses like routine, and any work should start with a warm-up, then the main part of the training, and a cool-down, whether at home or in the collecting ring at a competition. A dressage training session may only be needed twice a week if you are consistent with your aids and expectations when you ride your horse every day. Your horse should be ridden in a balanced and correct way of going all the time. When you initially start to work your horse you need to take time to warm up. In the winter this may be done with a rug on and the horse walked for ten to twenty minutes, allowing his muscles to warm up and take the weight of the rider. In the summer the temperature may be higher but the horse will still need time to loosen and stretch his muscles, and this will take at least ten minutes. This warm-up period can easily be done on a little walk around the lanes/ fields before schooling starts. Whilst quietly walking this is a good time for the rider to think and reflect about the aims and expectations

of the session. Horses learn by repetition and 'practice makes permanent', so take care that what you are asking your horse to do is what you want him to achieve.

Riders should also consider the need to warm up their own muscles and body: a rider who is stiff and tight in their own back will be unable to influence the horse positively. The rider should take time to address their positional strengths and weaknesses before they expect their horse to carry them. With a

Fig. 3.11   Horse stretching.

rider who is potentially stiff, cold or nervous it may be prudent to extend the walking warm-up period until both horse and rider have loosened up.

After the horse and rider have warmed up, a contact should be taken up and the horse asked to come into a rounder outline as the work is taken forward to trot. Initially the trot should be forward and free so the rider is likely to work in rising trot at this stage. The individual horse's temperament may influence the tempo of the initial work: thus a lazy horse may be asked to work a little 'up tempo' to encourage a quicker response to the rider's aids, whilst a 'hot' horse may be asked to work more slowly to encourage more relaxation. Either way the horse should feel comfortable to go forwards and accept the rider's leg and hand aids to develop the connection and suppleness through the body.

Once the horse is moving freely forwards, then the same principles can be carried out in the canter work; the rider should sit in a light seat to initially encourage the horse to be forward and soft over his back.

The horse needs to be able to go forward in a balanced and relaxed manner in walk, trot and canter. It is quite normal that there are differences to the horse's way of going between the left and right rein, but the aim is to minimize these inequalities and allow the horse to become more equal in his ridden work on both reins.

Relaxation and stretching should always be a part of the horse's work. In Fig. 3.11 the horse has been given a longer rein and the rider is asking him to take the rein forward and down whilst still maintaining a contact: this encourages him to relax and work freely through and over the back. This type of work should be used in the general training session, at the beginning as part of the warm-up, at the end during the cooling-off period, and if the horse becomes tight or tense in his general trot work.

BASIC TRAINING EXERCISES

The following exercises are a suggestion of some training movements that would improve the education of any horse working at British Dressage Novice level; this would include all the British Eventing tests up to and including Novice level. Transitions are an integral part of any horse's training and should be included frequently whenever the horse is being schooled. Additional exercises that improve the suppleness and consequently the contact and the horse's balance are leg-yielding and counter canter. These movements are not necessarily required within the tests, but are training movements that will enhance the horse's general way of going and so improve his balance, responses and ultimately his competition performance.

Exercise 1: Transitions

Once the horse is able to maintain a correct rhythm and a suitable tempo for his way of going in all paces, he can then develop his work to use more transitions. Transitions are paramount to the training of the horse as they assess his ability to change his balance between and within the paces. They are needed from the Novice horse right through to the Advanced competition horse. Although they are judged in the dressage phase within eventing, transitions are integral to the horse's education for show-jumping, cross-country or pleasure riding.

The aims of the exercise are as follows:

- To have the horse forward thinking, active and relaxed in understanding and accepting the rider's aids.
- To maintain and improve the horse's balance so he remains 'on the bit' throughout the transition.

Fig. 3.12   Transitions in corners, circles and straight lines.

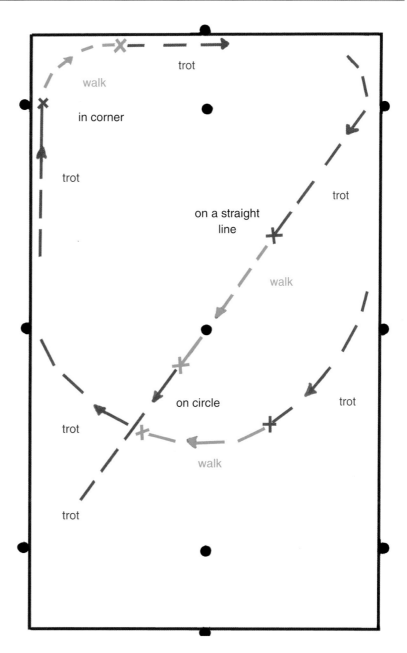

- To improve the quality of the basic paces and the transitions.

The exercise may be developed as follows:

- Starting in trot, approach the corner of the school: using a half halt, ride forwards to walk as you enter the corner; establish the rhythm and quality of the walk, and ride from three to seven steps. On leaving the corner, apply the leg for an upward transition to trot; establish the balance of the trot. Repeat in the next corner, and repeat on both reins to establish lateral suppleness.

*Fig. 3.13
Approaching
the corner in a
shortened trot.*

*Fig. 3.14   In the
corner, walking.*

*Fig 3.15   Coming
out of the corner,
transition to trot.*

The rider's responsibility is as follows:

- The rider needs to be in balance before entering the corner: their weight needs to be in the inside stirrup so that they are sitting with more weight through the inside leg.
- Ride forwards through the half halt by squeezing the outside rein to ask the horse to listen to the hand and 'pause' within the pace; on acceptance of this apply the inside leg to ask the horse to move forwards from his inside hind, thus establishing the half halt and priming the horse's attention for the transition.
- To ride forwards to walk, the downward aids are applied in plenty of time before the corner to ask the horse to take the weight on to the hind leg and push forward to walk.
- As the horse takes up walk, keep a soft inside hand as he has to turn to the inside by the nature of the corner; the outside hand should keep the contact to maintain the connection and balance through the turn.
- On completion of the walk through the corner, apply the forward driving aids from the inside leg to ask the horse to step upwards into trot. The outside rein maintains the connection and supports the balance through the transition.
- The rider should maintain their posture and balance throughout the corner and the transitions, allowing the horse to move forward from their leg to their hand, following the principles in the Scales of Training.

In the sequence of pictures opposite these upward and downward transitions are clearly depicted. In Fig. 3.13 the rider has taken sitting trot in preparation for the walk transition. The horse has responded by staying in balance but slightly shortening his

stride as he is about to make the transition to walk as he goes through the corner.

In Fig. 3.14 the horse has responded positively to the rider's aids and has stepped forward into a clearly defined four-beat walk. He remains on the bit and is taking the rein forward with a soft back (note the relaxed, raised tail position, free from tension).

In Fig. 3.15 the rider has now applied the trot aids and the horse has responded by moving freely through the transition into a balanced working trot.

Problem Solving

- **The horse comes against the hand into the downward transition and falls on the forehand.**
  Confirm that the horse is accepting the inside leg when in working trot around the school: on touching the horse with the leg, he should move freely forward. Check that the rider is in balance, with the leg correctly positioned with a vertical stirrup leather and not gripping upwards. If the horse is lazy to the correct leg aid, this needs to be backed up by the schooling whip behind the rider's inside leg to establish his acceptance of the driving aids. Maintain the contact and the soft feel through the inside rein, establish the connection through the outside rein, and then apply the leg aid to ride the horse forward. Often the horse comes heavy into the contact due to the lack of energy and activity in the hind leg. If the horse supports himself through the rider's hand, then the rider should soften the inside rein and ride forwards from the leg to energize the hind leg and re-establish the balance.
- **Inactivity through the transition.**
  Make sure that you are not riding too tight into the corner: the curve through the turn needs to be appropriate to the balance and education of the horse and

should follow a quarter turn of an 8m circle. Re-establish the acceptance of the leg aids before executing the exercise, and then support the transition with the schooling whip if required.

● **Overreaction to the transition.**
If the horse overreacts on the application of the upward aids and takes canter, he should not be told off because he has answered the question of listening and reacting to the rider's aids but a little too enthusiastically. He should be quietly brought forwards to trot and on the next corner the rider should take a little more time in applying the upward aids to maintain the desired transition through trot.

● **Jogging.**
Jogging is not a pace, and the horse should be quietly brought back to walk as soon as possible. He may be showing some signs of tension and anticipation in the downward transition. Make sure that the rider is sitting in balance and has not taken too much contact through the reins, encouraging the horse to pull and lose balance. If the horse jogs he should be asked to slow down and establish a correct and quiet walk before being asked to take trot. This may take several steps – the number is not important in this instance, but the quality of the walk must be established before the trot aid is applied.

Exercise 2: Leg Yield

Horses often lack balance in their early training and education and tend to use the walls for security or fall in through the turns and corners. This lack of balance increases through the paces, with the canter feeling particularly insecure. The cause of the insecurity is the lack of understanding and acceptance of the rider's inside leg and the connection to the outside rein. The horse's balance will improve once he is able to accept and be supported by the inside leg – that is, to yield to the rider's leg pressure.

The aims of the exercise are as follows:

● To develop looseness in the horse's body through lateral submission.
● To develop and secure the connection to the outside rein.
● To increase the responsiveness to the rider's aids.
● To encourage the horse to take more weight on to the inside hind leg as an introduction towards collection.

The exercise may be developed as follows:

● This exercise is the first step to lateral work and working on two tracks. It needs to be established before moving on to other exercises such as shoulder-in, travers and half-pass. The horse moves freely forwards and sideways on two tracks with slight head and neck flexion away from the direction of travel.
● The inside legs step forwards and cross over in front and across the outside feet. The flexion is always around the rider's leg that the horse is moving away from, regardless of where the movement is performed (from an inside track to the wall, from the outside wall to an inner track, or across the diagonal). The outside legs move away from the body to travel sideways. The regularity of the steps must be maintained throughout.
● Initially the horse's preference to move to the wall can be utilized. In walk, ride on to the three-quarter line, and after a few steps of going straight, apply the inside leg, asking the horse to step forwards and sideways. As soon as the horse has understood and accepted the aids he should be ridden forwards on to a straight line again. When initially teaching this exercise it is the quality of the

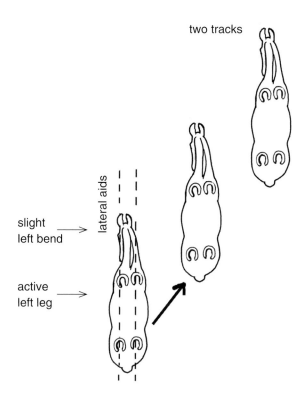

two tracks

lateral aids

slight
left bend

active
left leg

Fig. 3.16   Left leg yield.

steps and not the number that should be considered. Once established in walk on both reins, then repeat and develop into trot. The exercise can then be developed from the wall moving into the school. When the horse is secure and confident in this exercise, it can be developed on the diagonal, with the introduction of a canter transition on completion of the lateral movement. A shallow diagonal line can be ridden initially from the centre line to a quarter marker as in some British Dressage tests. Once this is achieved, the exercise should be developed to ride from one quarter marker to another across the diagonal of the school.

The rider's responsibility is as follows:

- The rider must be able to coordinate their aids whilst maintaining their own independent position. Ensure that their position is straight and with equal feel and acceptance in both reins.
- The rider needs to take more weight into the inside leg, feeling that they are sitting to that side of the saddle, with their outside seatbone feeling more to the centre of the saddle.
- The inside rein should have enough contact to encourage the flexion away from the direction of travel. Take care not to bring the inside contact across the neck so that it acts as an indirect rein aid: rather, it should be in a slightly outward, positioning direction. It may help to keep the inside elbow closer to the body with the thumb of the inside hand turning outwards to maintain the position suggested.
- To keep the inside leg active, slightly turn out the inside knee and keep the aids effective in a pulsing manner, keeping the heel low. The leg aid should be applied, released and reapplied as the horse reacts and steps away from the pressure. Avoid gripping up and keeping the leg fixed to the horse's side as he then has no opportunity to yield from the pressure and react to the leg aid.
- The outside aids still need to be applied to maintain the straightness through the body. Maintain an even contact with the outside rein to control the shoulder. Keep an active outside leg close to the girth to maintain the regularity and forwardness of the movement.

Problem Solving

It is quite all right to allow the tempo to slow down when initially training this exercise in order to develop the quality of the movement.

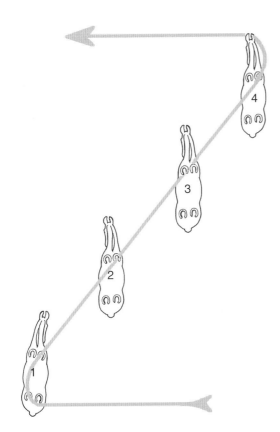

Fig. 3.17 Leg yield across the diagonal to canter.

Once established, then the steps may be energized with the outside leg.

Exercise 3: Trot and Canter Transitions

Transitions are a necessary and important aspect of every horse's training and can be developed once the horse is capable of working in an established manner within each of the three basic paces. Transitions are assessed throughout the dressage tests in the individual movements, but also in the collectives by how the horse can move from one pace to another (in the 'Impulsion' and 'Submission' marks).

The aims of the exercise are as follows:

● To encourage the horse to push forwards through the hind legs in the upward transitions.
● To encourage the horse to take more weight on to the hind legs in the downward transitions.
● To increase the response and reaction from the horse to the rider's aids.
● To develop the connection from the rider's leg to the contact throughout the transition.
● To maintain the rhythm, balance and quality of the paces through the transition.

The exercise may be developed as follows:

● The rider must have an independent position in both rising and sitting trot. When moving from rising to sitting, the rhythm and balance of the trot should be constant as the horse is able to accept the rider's weight.
● Riding a 20m circle, the rider takes sitting trot and quietly brings the outside leg back to ask the horse to strike off with the outside hind. The rider maintains the contact, but may have a little more weight in the outside rein to allow the horse to work forward to the rein while staying connected to the hand and 'on the bit'. In this way it is not solely the leg aid that initiates the canter but also the weight and movement of the outside seatbone and rider's shoulder keeping the weight consistent. The horse should pick up on the change in the rider's balance, and take up canter.
● Once the canter has been established and the horse is working in good balance, the rider can prepare for a trot transition. A more central posture is taken, with the outside shoulder being allowed to come more forward so the

rider has a straighter position. The rider should think about bringing their weight back and up by lifting the shoulders and taking the weight of the contact more into the elbows than the hand. The rider asks through the use of the half halt for the horse to bring the weight back. By maintaining the half-halt aids the horse will then naturally push forward into the trot.

- Staying on the circle, repeat the exercise until the transitions are secure and

Fig. 3.18   Canter transition from trot.

Fig. 3.19   Canter transition, second step.

Fig 3.20   Canter second stride.

confident, and maintain their quality. Once achieved, the exercise can be developed around the school in any direction.

The rider's responsibility is as follows:

● To sit in balance and maintain their position within the transitions, but also in the paces themselves.
● The rider must make sure they are sitting to the inside with a soft inside leg in order that the horse's inside hind is free to take the weight once the strike-off into canter has been made; this will support the connection over the back and help the horse to stay round and 'through' in the transition. The rider's weight should remain still, with the outside shoulder coming back.

In Figs 3.18–3.20 the upward transition into canter is clearly depicted. In Fig. 3.18 the horse has been ridden freely forward in sitting trot in preparation for the canter transition. His head is just in front of the vertical, but he is still taking the contact forward and is soft through his back.

In Fig. 3.19 the horse has taken the first canter step with his outside hind: he is now in the second phase, with the inside diagonal pair of legs on the ground. His outline is good for a horse working at novice level, although he has slightly drawn back in his neck.

In Fig. 3.20 the horse is just starting the second canter stride, with the outside leg being placed on the ground and the inside diagonal pair of legs in flight. The horse is appearing to work in a positive uphill manner due to the correct engagement of the hind legs, which are taking the weight underneath the horse, with good hock action.

Problem Solving

● **Running through the transition.**
  The rider needs to be more aware of the

quality of the trot, and should maintain the contact to prevent the trot from lengthening, which will cause the horse to lose his balance and come on to his shoulders. The rider needs to keep an active leg to maintain the energy of the trot without developing any more speed.

● **Incorrect lead.**
  The rider has lost balance, or has changed the flexion and directional balance of the horse through the contact. They should re-establish the balance and independence of their position. It may be helpful to ask for the upward transition approaching a corner in order to support the directional balance of the horse.

● **Becoming hollow.**
  The horse has initiated the canter through the shoulder rather than from the hind leg, and 'hops' into canter. The rider needs to energize the hind leg through support from a schooling whip in order to create a quicker response to the aids and to keep the horse forward thinking.

● **Loses energy into the downward transition.**
  Sometimes losing energy is more apparent with the lazier horse that drops off the rider's leg. The rider must make sure that when using the half halt they keep the forward driving aids and think of riding canter towards a medium trot transition.

Exercise 4: Counter Canter

The following counter canter exercises will help supple and straighten the horse, and so develop the balance and quality of the true canter.

The aims of the exercises are as follows:

● To make the horse supple on both reins equally, thus improving the balance and straightness of the canter.

● To improve the balance of the canter by developing the engagement of the inside hind leg and so lightening the shoulders.

The exercises may be developed as follows:

● True canter is when the horse is cantering on the same rein as the leading leg:

it should be established and correct, maintaining a regular three-beat footfall, and the horse should be secure to the canter aids on both reins. The canter should be adjustable, in that the horse should be able to lengthen and shorten the steps, thereby working towards collection of the pace: this will enhance

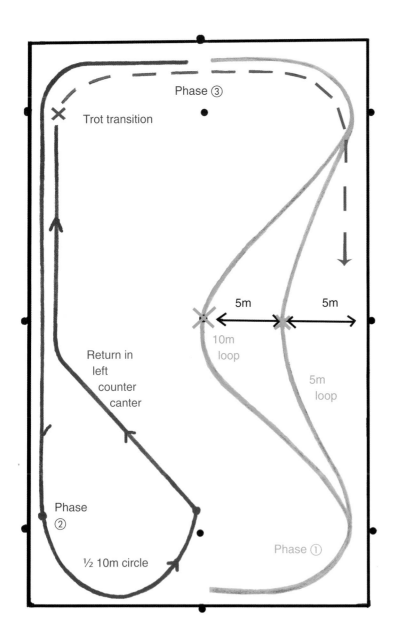

Fig. 3.21 Counter canter exercises.

the balance and ease of the canter through the directional changes. The rider's aids are the same as for true canter, but he must be even more aware of his balance, being sure to keep the weight through and down the inside leg.

- Phase One: The rider should be able to ride canter loops (5 to 10m) down the long side with no change in the balance and quality of the canter – the bigger the loop the harder it is to maintain the counter canter.
- Phase Two: In true canter, ride a 10 to 15m half circle at the quarter marker at the top end of the school, and return to the track in the middle of the school at about E or B. The counter canter positioning should be held – that is, with the flexion over the leading leg – until the far quarter marker, then make a transition to trot.
- Phase Three: When the horse is able to half circle and return to the quarter marker on both reins without losing balance or rhythm, then the counter canter can be developed to continue through the short side of the school; however, take care not to go too deep into the corners as the horse may lose balance, and so too the quality of the canter.
- When the horse is able to maintain a good quality, balanced counter canter through the short side, the canter can be continued working large and in time asking the horse to work deeper into the corners.
- Phase 4: The well established horse can then progress to cantering a figure of eight: canter a 20m circle in true canter at one end of the school, then through X change the direction to canter a 20m circle at the other end, but without changing the lead so this whole circle is in counter canter. This progression

of the counter canter exercise requires the horse to be able to maintain good balance and some degree of collection within the canter. The rider must also be able to ride the circles accurately in order to position the horse correctly and support the required changes in direction and balance.

The rider's responsibility is as follows:

- The rider must be independent and secure in their position to maintain the correct positional influence when riding counter canter: take care to keep the weight through the inside leg as it is easy to collapse the hips and allow the weight to slip to the outside. The rider's balance must be established to be independent of the horse so that they can maintain their balance too.
- The rider needs to be independent of the contact so they can soften the inside rein and allow the balance and flexion to be maintained through their position. The rider needs to keep the outside leg back behind the girth to maintain the energy and push of the horse's outside hind leg.
- Progression through the counter canter exercises must be made slowly. Make any directional changes gradually, and only when the horse is confident and secure in the preceding counter canter exercises.

Problem Solving

- **The horse becomes crooked.**
  The rider needs to be sure of their position, and must take care only to ask for the degree of straightness that is appropriate for the horse's education. If the horse is falling in (through the outside shoulder) or taking the inside legs

in away from the straight line, then the rider needs to take more contact through the outside rein and ask for less inside bend. This will straighten the horse's body and allow him to take more weight on to his inside hind.

● **The horse breaks into trot.**
The horse will trot if he loses balance, when either the rider has become over-ambitious regarding the depth of the corners, or more often they have lost their own balance to the outside and cannot maintain a correct position, becoming crooked themselves.

● **The horse loses the quality of the canter.**
If the energy of the canter is lost then the rider can maintain counter canter whilst working large and then ask for some medium canter on the long sides of the school, rebalancing the canter before the corner to establish the quality. At any point in the exercise if the quality is deteriorating then true canter should be re-established and used to energize the horse's basic way of going in his canter work, then return to the exercise and re-establish the counter canter work.

4 Show-Jumping Training

THE CANTER

The most important aspect of show-jumping training is the canter. Although the event horse still needs to have the skills and co-ordination to jump from both trot and gallop, he must show-jump out of a canter. The canter therefore needs to be correct, and, as for the dressage phase, the horse should be working to the Scales of Training. Most importantly the rhythm should be consistent, in a pure three-time footfall and showing a clear moment of suspension.

As the horse is required to jump a variety of fences across a range of ground conditions, the importance of the canter and the variations within the pace, combined with the horse's fitness, cannot be overstated. The horse needs to be able to lengthen and shorten the stride whilst maintaining the rhythm, balance and quality of the pace. The horse needs to shorten the canter on his approach to fences that are on turns and curves or that require more collection, such as uprights, and to lengthen it and cover more ground in order to jump through more open distances and fences such as spreads.

All show-jumping tracks are based upon the course designer building on distances that work around a 3.5m (4yd, 12ft) canter stride. Therefore, the training of the show-jumping phase should be based on the horse producing a working canter that covers this distance: being able to do so is critical through doubles of one and two strides, and any related distances that are three strides and over. The rider, having walked the course, should be able to work out the distance between related fences, and therefore the number of strides between them. If, through the training of the horse at home, the rider is confident that the horse can work within these distances, then this horse and rider combination is more likely to achieve a clear round.

TACK AND EQUIPMENT

A jumping saddle should be used for schooling over fences. It is important that the rider can shorten the stirrup length in order to maintain an independent balance when jumping and working in what is known as the 'light' or 'two-point' seat. A jumping saddle is a worthy investment, as a general purpose (GP) saddle does not support the increased flexion and the more forward position of the knee when the stirrups are shortened. It is quite realistic to compete in all three eventing phases in a jumping saddle, so this should be the primary investment in the tack and equipment that is needed to ride safely and effectively in all the phases of an event. When jump schooling the rider should ride with the stirrups at jumping length, as riding short will establish the rider's positional balance and support their fitness for this phase.

Many horses behave differently when they are being ridden at home as compared to when they are at a competition, and it is not unusual for them to need a different bit or piece of tack at an event because they can become

RIDER POSITION FOR JUMPING

Figs. 4.1–4.3 show clearly the shorter stirrup length and the lighter seat needed for jumping. In Fig. 4.1 the rider is demonstrating the correct length of stirrup for jumping when in halt. When adjusting the stirrups it is quite normal for them to feel short when in halt, but they should feel better when you are actually cantering and riding in a lighter seat. The hip and the heel are along the same vertical line, and the stirrup leather is also hanging vertically. The rider could allow her foot to come further forward into the stirrup as this would improve her balance once the horse starts to move.

In Fig. 4.2 the rider has a secure lower leg with a soft knee, allowing the weight to come through to the stirrup. She is then able to ride in balance with a soft hand when the horse is moving freely in canter. Ideally she could be looking up a little more in the direction of travel.

In Fig. 4.3 the rider is standing upright in the stirrups. This is a balance exercise to determine that the rider is able to ride independently from the horse and in particular independent from the contact. The rider has pushed her hips forward so that the weight is transferred through the whole of the leg. The hips, knees and ankles remain soft, allowing the joints to move and absorb the movement of the horse. The stirrups are hanging down vertically, with the widest part of the rider's foot placed on the stirrup iron. She is very upright in her position and is looking forward in the direction of travel. Once this independence is achieved, the rider can then quietly lower their weight back into the saddle and ride in a full or a light seat.

Fig. 4.1   Jumping position in halt.

Fig. 4.2 Light seat in canter.

Fig. 4.3 Standing seat in canter.

stronger or react in a different way when in a competitive situation. If this is the case, once you have found out which bit or piece of tack is the most effective, then this bridle can be kept for competitions and a 'general' bridle used for training. Most important is that the tack and equipment used must fit correctly, and be fitted firmly enough to work effectively: all too often a noseband is too loose or a bit too low, and this will be more antagonistic to the horse than the actual choice of tack.

The horse in Fig. 4.4 is suitably tacked up for jumping with a Mexican grakle and running martingale. The grakle is fitted so that the nose strap lies above the projecting cheek bones, then comes forward over the nose where it

crosses, and is then fitted under the chin groove where it is secured. In this picture the horse is alert and standing with her head up, thus making the running martingale look taut on the rein. When fitted, these straps should reach up to the top of the neck, which allows plenty of movement for general work.

The Training Session

When schooling for show-jumping it is important to start the training session with a stirrup length that is suitable for jumping. The majority of people ride too long and consequently lack balance and independence

Fig. 4.4 Grakle noseband and running martingale.

when jumping or when having to deal with problems that occur in the course of a show-jumping round. The rider should have a stirrup length that allows them to have a soft, flexed knee, with the heel below the level of the stirrup, and maintaining a vertical line through the stirrup leather (see panel overleaf).

The rider should warm up the horse in the same way as for general training on the flat, with the exception that they will be working in their jumping saddle with a shorter stirrup length, which may be a couple of holes shorter than when riding on the flat. When initially taking up canter, the rider should adopt a light seat and focus on the quality of the canter, and also their own position and the security of their lower leg.

This is an excellent time to consider the rider's own balance, co-ordination and fitness. As much as five minutes can be spent in warming up the horse in the canter work, and the rider should have the strength, co-ordination and fitness to maintain an independent and balanced position whilst doing this. If the rider has only one horse to ride then this warm-up phase has the added bonus of supporting and increasing the rider's fitness for both show-jumping and cross-country work. The rider needs to focus on maintaining a secure independent lower leg, without the need to keep resting by sitting on the horse's back. The contact should be independent of the reins. If the rider is struggling to maintain this independence then the warm-up should be carried out by holding on to a neck strap until they have developed their fitness and security of position to be independent of the horse.

When both horse and rider have warmed up in all three paces, the horse should be allowed to have a rest, his girth should be checked and any required adjustments made to tack and clothing. Before commencing any jumping the rider should then develop the canter work to improve the range of ground cover in that pace, and the horse's acceptance of the aids.

The rider's responsibility to themselves and the horse is to set a suitable pace for the questions asked in the show-jumping course, and to ride a suitable line to maintain balance and rhythm. The horse's responsibility is to jump the fence out of this rhythm. The horse jumps any obstacle by addressing three main points: he looks at the obstacle, adjusts his balance to negotiate it, and then avoids what is placed in front of him by jumping over it. This principle is the same for a young horse jumping its first cross-pole or an advanced show-jumper approaching an oxer of maximum dimensions. In competition the rider has had the luxury of walking the course, hence they should be able to select and maintain a suitable line (the direction of travel to the fence) and pace (the speed of the approach) for the horse to be in a good position to negotiate the fences successfully and confidently.

Factors that the rider should think about when training for show-jumping are the demands of the level of competition (the height and spread of the fences), the type of fences to be jumped (verticals and oxers), as well as the shape, colour and construction of the fences (planks, gates, water trays, fillers, walls), the distances between the fences (turns and approaches, related distances and dog legs) and finally the ground conditions (whether the competition is indoors, outside, on an artificial surface, on grass, and any idiosyncrasies of the terrain).

Getting the Stride Right

If the rider produces a canter that maintains a rhythm and its balance then the horse can adjust his stride on the approach to the fence in order to clear the jump. The ability to meet the fence in a balanced and energized canter should be addressed through the canter between the fences. The horse should then be able to adjust and find his own stride whilst

THE IMPORTANCE OF A CORRECT LOWER LEG POSITION

Figs. 4.5–4.8 show clearly the effects of an incorrect and a correct lower leg position when riding on the flat between fences, and when actually jumping a fence.

In Fig. 4.5 the rider is cantering at her jumping length but has become tight in the knee. This allows the lower leg to draw up and grip in the calf, and she has thereby lost the depth and security of the lower leg gained by having her weight in the heel, in the stirrup iron. As a consequence her weight is in her seat, causing her to tip forwards on to her hands. Although the horse is in canter, he needs to be ridden more forwards to a longer rein and a more connected contact.

From the basis of the weakness in the lower leg on the flat, it is easy to see in Fig. 4.6 how the rider is unable to maintain a secure and independent position over the fence. On take-off she has turned her legs out and has braced through the knee, using her arms to support her position over the fence.

In Fig. 4.7 the horse is turning left, with both horse and rider looking in the direction of travel. The rider's weight is securely through the lower leg with a soft knee, and whilst the rider is sitting in the saddle, she is soft in her back, allowing the weight to come all the way through to the stirrup.

Fig. 4.8 clearly shows that due to the security of her lower leg on the flat, this rider can maintain an independent position over the fence. On the landing stride her weight is firmly in the stirrup with a soft knee, and her weight is above the horse, allowing him to use his head and neck freely to balance on landing. Both horse and rider are looking forward to the next fence.

Fig. 4.5
Incorrect lower leg on the flat.

Fig. 4.6 Incorrect lower leg when jumping.

Fig. 4.7 Correct lower leg on the flat.

Fig. 4.8 Correct lower leg when jumping.

jumping – an important skill, particularly in the event horse, which has to have some self-reliance when jumping across country. It should not be the rider's responsibility to find the stride when show-jumping until the higher levels (Intermediate and above) when the fences become far more demanding and involve more technical distances. If a rider feels uncomfortable about not being able to 'see' a stride, then a helpful exercise is to count aloud the canter strides into the fence.

The rider needs to be confident in developing a sense of feel for the rhythm, and this may vary between horses. Riders often want to 'do' something to help the horse, whereas keeping still and in balance is what the horse needs the rider to be able to do, and not suddenly change the stride and rhythm on the approach to the fence. By counting the strides to the jump the rider becomes aware that the horse will jump on a whole number and consequently jump out of his stride. It is also helpful to count upwards as sometimes the rider can count down and find that when counting three, two, one, the horse hasn't decided to jump and there is an extra stride!

Surfaces and Conditions

For many people the majority of the horse's training occurs on an artificial surface, but unless you are at a major event then the competitive show-jumping phase will be carried out on grass. Thus it is important that an active training plan is made to ensure some of the jump training takes place on grass in order to prepare both the horse and rider for dealing with the horse's reactions to a different and potentially variable surface.

Events are held from March right through to October, and generally carry on regardless of the weather. With this in mind, a rider should train in all circumstances so that the weather conditions do not have a negative impact on the horse's performance. It is good practice to ride when it is very hot, cold, windy and raining, as the rider will then be aware of how the horse reacts to the different weather conditions and can accommodate this in a competitive situation.

JUMPING EXERCISES

The following exercises are just a suggestion of some training exercises that would improve the skills and confidence of any horse jumping up to 1.10m. The ability to approach a fence in a good quality canter is imperative to allow the horse to jump. The rider is responsible for the line and the pace, and these exercises work on his ability to stay in balance and be responsible for those two aspects within the show-jumping phase.

It is important that the rider develops an awareness of the individual horse's rhythm and stride length to be able to adjust the stride and therefore ground cover, and also to sit in balance and allow the horse to jump out of his stride. Developing these aspects will help gain horse and rider confidence as well as the quality of the bascule on both curved and straight lines. All of these aspects are likely to be tested in the show-jumping phase and should improve the balance, responses and ultimately the competition performance of the horse.

Exercise 1: Canter Poles to a Single Fence

This exercise establishes an energetic canter that covers the ground with a stride length that is suitable for jumping. It encourages the rider to be aware of the quality of the canter that is needed before jumping a course of fences in a competition environment. Before starting this exercise the horse should be able to canter correctly, maintaining a three-time rhythm with a clear moment of suspension, whilst staying in balance through straight lines and circles. An incorrect canter may be four time, when the horse doesn't take a clean step with the inside diagonal legs and instead the inside hind strikes the ground first, breaking the diagonal phase: this results in a canter that lacks impulsion and is of poor quality.

The aims of the exercise are as follows:

- To establish a suitable jumping canter and support forward, straight riding through a line of poles to a fence.
- To help the rider become aware of the quality of the canter and the influence of correct turns to and away from the line of poles/fence.
- To allow the horse to jump out of his stride, developing confidence in his jumping.
- To allow the rider to influence the canter on the approach whilst allowing the horse to jump independently over the fences, whilst

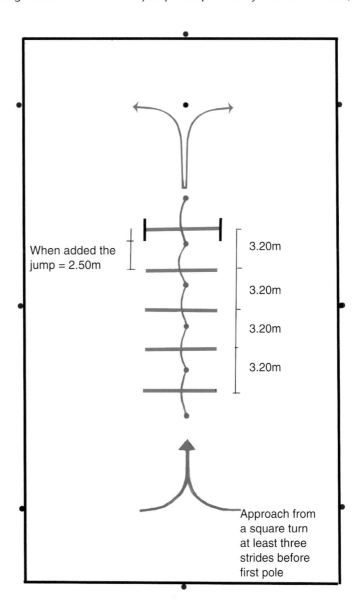

When added the jump = 2.50m

3.20m

3.20m

3.20m

3.20m

Approach from a square turn at least three strides before first pole

Fig. 4.9   Canter poles to single fence.

maintaining their own balance through the exercise.

The exercise may be developed as follows:

- Lay out five poles in a straight line with a distance of 3.2m between each. Place the poles so that the exercise can be ridden on both the left and right rein. Jump wings and extra poles can be placed at the end of the ground poles so the exercise may be developed to include a fence.
- Initially the canter should be established with the rider in a light seat and the horse maintaining a good rhythm on both reins. The rider then rides through the corner with a square turn and approaches the series of poles; maintaining the balance and rhythm, the horse should canter evenly and cleanly over all the poles.
- When he can do this in balance and quietly (not touching or knocking the poles), a small fence can be added at the end of the series of poles. The fence should be moved slightly closer (2.5m) to the fourth pole to support a closer take-off point when jumping. Initially a small upright should be built and the horse jumped through the grid maintaining the balance, rhythm and quality of the canter throughout.
- When this can be completed confidently, the fence can be raised, fillers may be added, and the fence increased to an ascending and then a true oxer as the horse and rider combination gain in confidence and skill, producing a quality canter, good bascule over the fence, and a balanced ride-away/exit of the exercise.
- The exercise should be repeated on both reins. If the rider approaches from the left rein then they should exit to the right, returning to approach from the right,

progress through the exercise and then exit to the left.

The rider's responsibility is as follows:

- To maintain their position and balance in the canter, through the turns, within the grid and through the landing and ride-away. They must look ahead of the exercise around the corner to ride a square turn to the line of poles/fences. The line to the poles should be straight from the turn, through the exercise and then continued forwards until the rider chooses to turn away to the left or right.
- To allow the horse the freedom and independence to jump and maintain the balance, bascule and rhythm throughout the exercise. The rider's position should remain constant, secure through the lower leg with a soft hand allowing the horse freedom to use his head and neck without the rider coming in front of or behind the movement. Some fold over the fence is expected without losing balance and security or negatively influencing the horse's balance.

Fig. 4.10 shows a good ride-away: this is the first complete stride as the horse and rider leave the fence, and both are looking forward in the direction of travel. The rider's weight is securely through the lower leg, in a light seat and a soft contact, ready to establish the quality of the canter for the next fence.

Problem Solving

- **The horse keeps hitting the poles.** Check that the distance between the poles is suitable for the horse: ideally he needs to learn to come through the exercise on an open stride. The rider needs to learn not to try to 'fix' the horse's problem, but should return to their responsibility of the canter, re-establishing the quality and only then returning to the exercise. Some horses may

Fig. 4.10   A good ride-away.

find the distance too long initially so it can be reduced, although once horse and rider are secure and confident in the exercise it should be re-established.

● **Changing the canter lead.**
The horse starts off in true canter, but as he progresses through the exercise he changes in front and/or behind; this is usually because he must overstretch to reach the last poles, and because in doing so he then loses engagement, he changes his canter lead. Often, too, the rider has leant forward, which makes it difficult for the horse to stay in balance and he then comes on to the forehand. The rider needs to maintain the impulsion through the canter, keeping the horse light in the hand and in an uphill balance. As the hind leg becomes more active through improved engagement the horse's balance will improve and he should be able to stay in true canter.

● **Lack of straightness.**
If the rider rides a curved line through the corner on the approach to the line of poles, as opposed to a square turn, the horse will

tend either to undershoot or to overshoot his line. Consequently the straightness through the horse's body is lost and he will drift across the poles or fall through the outside shoulder: horses that quicken to a fence will often fall in on the turn and 'load' their inside shoulder, whilst a lazy horse is more inclined to drift out. If the turn is the issue, then two poles placed parallel to each other out of the corner can help guide the horse and rider to a straighter line to the exercise. Either way the rider needs to establish a balanced, energetic canter to support the lateral suppleness and line to the poles, taking care to keep an even contact themselves so as not to increase the neck bend and allow the horse to lose straightness.

● **Poor bascule.**
If the horse is meeting the fence well and in good balance he should be able to 'look', 'adjust' and 'avoid' the fence through a suitable bascule at the point of take-off. Check that the distance between the last (fourth) pole and the fence is appropriate

for the horse, and if not, adjust it to allow a more balanced take-off point. Consider the design and construction of the fence: if the horse has jumped it successfully a few times then he may have become complacent, in which case the fence should be altered – the height or the width of the spread increased – so as to develop the horse's own focus and responsibility for the jump. Check that the balance of the rider's position has been maintained: if the rider comes in front of, or behind the movement, this can negatively affect the

horse's balance and consequently his shape or bascule over the fence.

Figs 4.11 and 4.12 show a comparison between a good bascule and a bad one, and the effect that this has on the rider's ability to ride effectively. In Fig. 4.11 the horse is making a lovely shape over the fence. The oxer allows the horse to stretch up and across the jump: he is equal in his front and hind legs, showing a relaxed appearance as he comfortably reaches the highest and widest point of the jump. The rider is sitting in balance, her hands lightly

Fig. 4.11   Good bascule.

placed in a forward crest release (i.e. her hands are following the movement up the horse's head towards the crest), allowing the horse to use his neck effectively to balance as he jumps. Her upper body is secure and independent of the horse. Her lower leg is in a good position, though ideally if the knee were turned out slightly the calf would be closer to the horse's side, giving the rider better security.

In Fig. 4.12 the horse is showing a very hollow and inverted frame as she is about to take off. Although the legs are all pairs and both horse and rider are straight, the horse's neck is raised causing the back to hollow. This tendency is not helped by the mare's conformation, but it can be improved by developing the quality of the canter on the approach to the fence. Because the horse is hollow it is difficult for the rider to be balanced: as a result she has drawn back with the contact and has herself become hollow in her back.

- **Poor finish/ride-away.**
  If the horse is enthusiastic on leaving the fence this could indicate that he likes his jumping; however, he still needs to be ridden away to a straight finish and the next turn. The landing is just as important as the take-off from a jumping aspect, as the landing stride becomes the first stride to the

Fig. 4.12 Poor bascule.

next fence, be it a double, related distance, or through a turn to another line of fences. The rider needs to consider their balance on landing, too: if they land heavily in the saddle then the horse will naturally react by hollowing and rushing away from the fence. They should land with their weight in the stirrup so as to maintain their posture, and to have a positive influence on riding away from the fence. If the horse quickens away from the fence the rider needs to bring their balance back without pulling too much on the reins: their weight should stay in the lower leg, and then be taken into the seat before using the contact. Their shoulders should be raised, and should not be positioned too far forward over the horse's wither, which would actively encourage the horse on to his shoulders and so put him out of balance.

Exercise 2: Canter on a Circle with Variation of Stride Length

This exercise helps the rider develop a feel for any change in the horse's canter stride length, and to measure this change; they can then progress to establishing a collected and a medium canter. It is also helpful for the rider to think of the qualities of the canter with regard to jumping: thus the medium canter should give the same feeling as the canter required to jump a parallel fence, and the collected canter as the canter needed for an upright fence.

The aims of the exercise are as follows:

- To have the horse forward thinking, active, responsive and accepting the rider's aids within the canter transitions.
- To establish a change in the tempo and stride length of the canter, and to adapt this awareness to the show-jumping environment.

- To maintain and improve the balance of both canters, relating this to the requirements when jumping.
- To improve the quality of the canters, and the rider's awareness of achieving this.

The exercise may be developed as follows:

- After warming up the horse, establish a 20m circle in working canter at one end of the school. The rider should count the number of canter strides that it takes to canter from the end of the school to crossing the centre line. This should be repeated a few times until an equal number of strides can be ridden in both halves.
- Once a regular number of strides has been established in each half, the rider should shorten the canter stride and reduce the ground cover as they return from the centre line towards the end of the school: this will add an extra stride or two in this half of the circle. The horse should remain in balance whilst taking more weight on to the hind leg.
- On crossing over the centre line at the end of the school, a transition within the pace should be made to ride forwards: this will increase the ground cover and lengthen the frame of the horse, thereby reducing the number of strides in this half of the circle. On approaching the centre line a transition should be made to shorten the frame to reduce the number of canter strides again.
- Repeat the exercise until the quality of the canter is consistent and the transitions are responsive and balanced. Change the rein and repeat.

The rider's responsibility is as follows:

- The rider needs to be in balance whilst establishing the canter: the weight needs to be in the inside stirrup so they can sit with more weight to the inside, thus supporting the balance and independence of the position.

- Keep the aids simple and explicit to the horse. To shorten the frame and increase the number of canter strides on the circle, the rider needs to prepare the horse before crossing the centre line with a half halt, then ask him to adjust his balance and take more weight on to his hind leg by using their own bodyweight as an aid: do this by sitting up tall from the waist to encourage more weight into the seat.

- On approaching the centre line at the bottom end of the school the rider needs to lighten the seat and quicken the leg to allow the horse to step forward and lengthen his frame. The rider may slightly lighten their seat to allow the horse to soften and lift through the back, or take rising canter.

- The rider should avoid using the hand to increase the contact in order to shorten the horse's frame, as this will only cause him to hollow, and thereby reduce the quality of

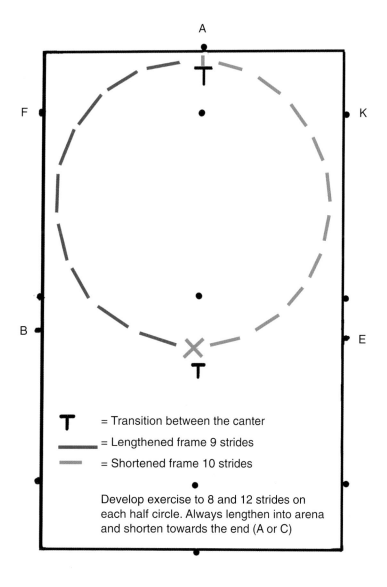

T = Transition between the canter

——— = Lengthened frame 9 strides

– – – = Shortened frame 10 strides

Develop exercise to 8 and 12 strides on each half circle. Always lengthen into arena and shorten towards the end (A or C)

Fig. 4.13 Canter on a circle.

Fig. 4.14 Shortened frame on a circle.

Fig. 4.15 Lengthened frame on a circle.

the canter, potentially causing the horse to lose balance and break into trot.

The two aspects of this exercise are shown clearly in Figs 4.14 and 4.15. Note that the rider is riding this exercise in her jumping saddle at her jumping length: this allows her to develop a similar feeling and response from the horse as when she is actually jumping. In Fig. 4.14 the horse's frame has been shortened, allowing the shoulders to lighten as more weight is placed on the hind leg and in particular the hock. Ideally the rider, although soft in her position, could be sitting a little more upright to encourage the horse to shorten his frame and consequently his stride length.

In Fig. 4.15 the horse has been allowed to lengthen through his neck whilst still remaining on the bit and taking the contact forward. His frame has been opened up, allowing the hind leg to push forward, thereby increasing the stride length and ground cover. The rider can sit lighter, taking her own weight off the horse's back, allowing him to remain round and forward in his canter.

Problem Solving

- **The horse comes against the hand when shortening and breaks into trot.** The rider has tried to shorten the frame by taking a stronger contact, anxious to 'slow' the horse down. However, it is important to increase the number of strides only very gradually, and without losing the quality of the canter: thus if the normal number of strides on the half circle is, for example, twelve, then it will be sufficient to ask for just thirteen when you first ask the horse to shorten and take more weight on his hind leg. When this can be achieved the rider can ask for fourteen strides, but only if the balance and quality of the canter are maintained.

It is quite acceptable to start by going from working canter to the shortened canter and back until the transition within the pace is achieved; then the exercise can be developed to work towards medium and collected canter.

- **Loss of balance in the transitions.** The rider needs to make sure that they have prepared for the transition early enough for the horse to understand the aids and have time to react to them. The aids should be applied consistently, but not necessarily together, so the horse can react to the forward driving aids for the development of the medium strides, or to the holding aids, through the rider's weight and seat, for the collected strides.

- **Loss of balance in the canter.** The horse has become unbalanced and is either falling on to the inside shoulder, escaping through the outside shoulder, or running on to the forehand: whatever the effect, he is losing balance because of the change in the stride pattern. First, re-establish the regular working canter with the same number of canter strides on each half of the circle; then ask the horse either to lengthen or shorten the strides whilst maintaining a correct, balanced canter. Ideally adjust the canter stride to the one that the horse finds easiest in order to improve the canter transition when returning to the working canter. When this is achieved, the canter can be developed and the number of strides to be shortened or lengthened increased.

Exercise 3: Jumping on a Circle

It is important to develop the horse's ability to jump out of a rhythm, whilst maintaining the balance and quality of the canter.

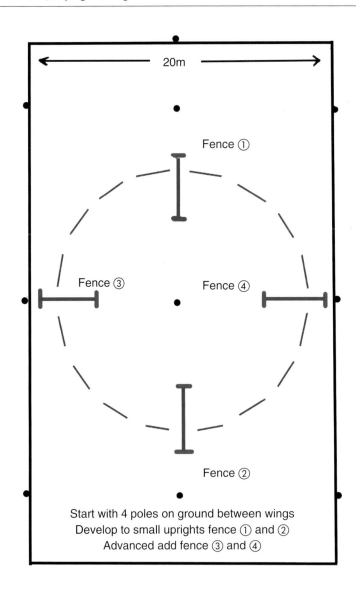

Fig 4.16 Jumping on a circle.

20m

Fence ①

Fence ③

Fence ④

Fence ②

Start with 4 poles on ground between wings
Develop to small uprights fence ① and ②
Advanced add fence ③ and ④

Educating both horse and rider to maintain the consistency of the canter will develop their confidence in being able to meet a fence in a good rhythm and with a balanced take-off.

The aims of the exercise are as follows:

- To develop a consistent rhythm whilst maintaining balance on the circle.
- To allow the horse to find his balance and jump out of his stride.

- To develop the rider's feel for the rhythm and allow the horse to jump.
- To help the rider establish an independent position whilst co-ordinating their aids to support the horse's balance.

The exercise may be developed as follows:

- Mark out a 20m circle with four fences set at the four tangent points off the circle. Initially the fences should be set up with a place pole between the wings. The rider should establish canter and aim to maintain the canter on the circle with the horse staying in rhythm whilst cantering between the wings and over the poles. The horse should canter between the poles with the same number of strides between each fence. When this is achieved on both reins the poles can be raised to become small fences.

Initially raise one of the poles to a small upright at about 75–90cm. Continue with the exercise, establishing the same number of strides between each of the wings. The fence should be an upright and not a cross-pole, as this allows the horse some adjustment on take-off without having to jump the high side of a cross-pole fence. Develop this on both reins.

● Raise the fence opposite the first jump to the same height and develop the exercise as before. Eventually the uprights may be raised to the height that the horse is comfortably competing at; repeat and develop the exercise on both reins.

● With the more advanced horse and rider, the third and fourth fences can be added into the exercise so that the horse has to jump a fence, land, maintain the same number of strides, and repeat over the next three fences. The exercise should be maintained for at least a couple of circles before the rider asks the horse to ride

Fig. 4.17   Canter on a circle: the approach …

ABOVE: **Fig. 4.18   ...the jump...**

BELOW: **Fig. 4.19   ...and the ride-away.**

out of the exercise on to a straight line away from the circle to finish.

Figs 4.17–4.19 show how this exercise improves the horse's rhythm and confidence. In Fig. 4.17 the rider has established the canter on the circle and has come over the pole on the ground, turning on the quarter circle to the small upright. Both horse and rider are looking forward to the fence, staying in a balanced, regular canter.

In Fig. 4.18 the horse has confidently jumped out of her canter stride, taking off and landing in right canter. The rider is looking forward to the next quarter, which will be a pole on the ground opposite the previous red and white pole.

In Fig. 4.19 the rider through their body language has turned on to the line of the circle with the horse landing in balance and able to follow the line of the circle, staying in rhythm within the quarter turn. The rider should then follow through and sit up in the next stride to support the horse's balance through the turn.

The rider's responsibility is as follows:

- To have an established, independent jumping position and be able to maintain their balance whilst riding on a circle. Their stirrups should be at a suitable length to allow the lower leg to be secure and stable whilst jumping.
- To support the balance and rhythm of the horse's canter by maintaining the co-ordination of the aids, and to keep the weight into the inside stirrup to allow the horse to stay true to the line of the circle. They can then maintain the horse's straightness on the circle by keeping the contact in the outside rein.
- To develop the adaptability of their position over the fence to re-establish

the rhythm on landing and to the next fence.

Problem Solving

- **The horse changes canter lead or goes disunited.**
  Maintain the canter through the quarters of the circle: when cantering over the next pole the horse is likely to change back to the correct lead. If very unbalanced, he may change to true counter canter. Maintain the canter and the bend and use the next set of poles to encourage the horse to change back to true canter. This can be helped by using an open inside rein as the horse takes off, to encourage him to land with the correct lead and in balance.
- **The horse loses balance through the quarter turns.**
  The rider needs to focus on maintaining their position to support the balance, line and straightness on the circle. As the horse jumps the fence, the rider should look ahead to the next fence to support their positional balance. At this point it is important to keep proceeding through the exercise. If the rider leaves the circle and rides away on a straight line, then the purpose of the exercise is lost. Maintain the canter on the circle and allow the horse to re-establish his balance and line. If the quality of the work is lost, then take a step back to a single fence or poles on the ground until the balance and quality are re-established.
- **The horse drifts out through the shoulder.**
  Initially this is likely to be the horse drifting out to make more room for the take-off point at the jump. As the quality and balance of the canter improve, and the horse is able to jump out of the rhythm, the straightness should also improve as the horse learns to become

more conservative and economical in his jump technique.

Exercise 4: Jumping Lines

Horse and rider should be comfortable jumping related distances, and the horse should have the confidence to listen to the rider so that straight and curved lines can be ridden.

The aims of the exercise are as follows:

● To maintain the rhythm and balance of the canter when jumping single and related fences.
● To teach the rider to focus on riding forwards to the next fence.
● To help the rider establish a suitable canter and maintain the balance and rhythm between fences.

The exercise may be developed as follows:

● Set up the exercise with an oxer on a straight line, and two uprights set up on a dog leg on a related distance of five to six strides.
● Once the horse has been sufficiently worked in on the flat he can be warmed up over an upright and then a small oxer. When jumping the oxer the initial focus should be on the quality of the canter, and the approach and exit from the fence. When jumping in a good balance the exercise can progress to adding the related fences.
● Initially, to support the balance of the horse, the rider can approach the oxer on the left rein, land and then ride forward a couple of strides before turning left to the upright on the dog leg. This can then be repeated on the other rein, approaching from the right rein and turning right.
● The exercise can progress to jumping from one rein (left) and then turning to the

other (right). Once developed, the lines can be jumped in reverse, linking the fences together – for example, the oxer to the left-handed upright, and then turning right, return over the right-handed upright and turn left to the oxer.
● Various lines and combinations can then be put together.

The rider's responsibility is as follows:

● The rider needs to be in balance whilst establishing the canter on the approach to the first fence; their weight should be central, so they can land and ride forwards on to a straight line, thus supporting the balance and independence of their position.
● The rider should sit straight on landing, and then ask the horse to make a change in direction to approach the dog leg to the left or the right of the centre line.
● The rider needs to maintain or quickly re-establish the quality of the canter and the balance of the horse between the fences.

Figs. 4.21–4.23 show how this exercise works. In the first picture the rider has made a good approach and landing over the first fence – although she is a little left of centre, albeit straight. Nevertheless, from this position she can choose to ride forward in a straight line, or turn left or right to either of the other fences.

In Fig. 4.22 she has turned to the left, and is maintaining a straight line to the fence, establishing the quality of the canter between the fences. The horse is approaching in left canter, in good balance.

What we do one way, we should do the other: in Fig. 4.23 the rider has chosen to turn right after the first upright, and, as before, both horse and rider are looking in the direction of travel, and the horse is cantering on the right lead.

Fig. 4.20 Jumping lines.

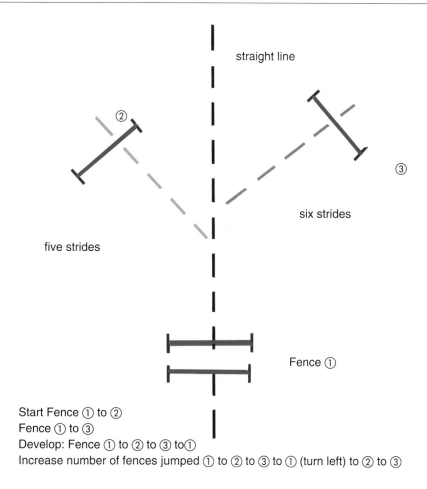

straight line

②

③

six strides

five strides

Fence ①

Start Fence ① to ②
Fence ① to ③
Develop: Fence ① to ② to ③ to①
Increase number of fences jumped ① to ② to ③ to ① (turn left) to ② to ③

Problem Solving

- **The horse falls in towards the second fence.**
  The rider needs to keep straight as they approach the second fence, taking care not to collapse in their position. The horse is likely to fall on to the inside shoulder on his stiffer side. The rider should focus on riding the horse forwards from the oxer and then riding a squarer turn to the second fence, maintaining the contact through the outside rein and riding the horse forwards around the inside leg.

- **The horse drifts out and loses the outside shoulder.**
  This is likely to happen as the horse turns to the fence on his softer side. The rider should land after the oxer and focus on the quality of the canter as soon as possible, supporting the balance through the turn and not allowing the horse to quicken and lose the straightness to the second fence.

- **The horse rushes to the fence and anticipates the exercise.**
  Make sure that the horse is listening to the aids, and keep the exercise fresh by changing direction and sometimes simply jumping each of the fences on its own, focusing on the quality of the canter both to and away from the fence, as well as the straightness. In addition, make sure that the rider is not getting in front of the movement, thereby encouraging the horse to quicken on landing because they have lost their balance.

Fig. 4.21   Landing straight…

Fig. 4.22   …turning left…

Fig. 4.23   …and turning right.

5 Cross-Country Training

The cross-country phase tests stamina and skill, and the relationship between the horse and rider, and how well they are able to negotiate their way around a series of fences designed to blend into the terrain of the land. The jumping efforts are related to the level of education of the horse, and the demands increase as the horse and rider progress through the levels of competition.

Both horse and rider need to develop the skills and fitness that will enable them to have the balance and co-ordination required when working up, down, across a hill or galloping on the flat. Modern training and the extent to which riders depend on working on an artificial surface can give a false sense of security and fitness levels to both the horse and the rider, and it is critical that both horse and rider undertake some training out of the school environment in order to develop the skills and confidence to canter, gallop and jump in open country in a variety of ground conditions. The great British weather will undoubtedly mean that when competing it will often be necessary to jump when it is raining, windy or hot, and when the ground is wet, boggy, muddy and/or hard.

RIDER POSITION AND FITNESS

The rider needs to develop an independent position so they can accommodate the changes in ground conditions and any variations of gradient, and can move with the horse so he can jump the fences safely and efficiently. They are also responsible for their own fitness and balance, because it is unfair to expect the horse to carry an unbalanced rider who is fatigued towards the end of a cross-country course: such lack of fitness is likely to negatively influence the horse's own fitness and performance, ultimately causing fatigue and injury, and possibly even leading to a fall. It is therefore entirely the rider's responsibility to make sure that both they and their horse are fit enough to compete safely and successfully.

The rider needs to make sure that their stirrup length is short enough to allow them flexion through the knee in order to move independently in the saddle when jumping. They must maintain an independent jumping position when riding across the country, and should train at their cross-country stirrup length, or even a hole or two shorter, in order to develop their own fitness and condition in training. It is often safer for the rider to sit slightly behind the movement over a fence than to get in front of the centre of balance, and to do this they rely upon the position and security of their lower leg in order to be stable and independent of the horse when jumping. Their weight should drop through the lower leg and into the heel, and not be pinned into the knee, which would allow the lower leg to swing backwards as the horse goes over a fence. By keeping the weight in the stirrup iron the rider can maintain a secure lower leg and consequently better balance over a fence and on landing. This is particularly important if the

Fig. 5.1 Tall rider's stirrups at cross-country length.

Fig 5.2 Shorter rider's stirrups at cross-country length.

horse should twist or leave a leg when jumping an obstacle.

Figs 5.1 and 5.2 show two riders of different build with their stirrups at cross-country length. In Fig. 5.1 the rider is naturally tall and long in the leg, but her position is well balanced. She could possibly ride a little shorter, but this is limited by the design of the saddle which prevents her knee from coming into the saddle flap. She can, however, clear the front of the pommel comfortably.

The rider in Fig. 5.2 has a rounder thigh, and is also on a horse with a bigger frame, but she has plenty of room in the saddle to move her weight forward and back to the cantle to accommodate her balance when jumping. However, her weight has come into her knee, which does reduce the security of her lower leg, and she needs to address this fault in order to develop greater effectiveness and influence in her position when going cross country.

BE PREPARED

Relaxed and ready for a cross-country session! The riders are wearing the equipment they would compete in so they can check on fit and comfort, right down to medical cards and stopwatches. Although these are not required for schooling it is good practice to make sure all your equipment fits well, and is comfortable, safe and secure. It should not be left to the day of the competition to find out that your armband keeps falling down!

Fig. 5.3   Horses and riders suitably turned out for going across the country.

The Jumping Saddle

The design of the saddle is of equal importance in that it must allow the rider to fold at the hips and move their seat backwards, so they can move their weight backwards when needed without losing the security of the lower leg. The saddle must also be sufficiently forward cut that the rider's knee is secure when riding in the two-point position or the light seat. The least suitable saddle to compete in is the general purpose (GP) saddle, as the limited knee roll makes it impossible for the rider to ride short enough and so to move independently when needed.

Saddles come in many shapes and sizes, but it is most important that a saddle fits both the horse and the rider. A jumping saddle is the best and also the safest saddle in which to ride across the country, and at the lower levels of competition it is quite acceptable to compete in the dressage phase in a jumping saddle: this should therefore be the most important single investment that the rider makes. Some saddles come with a single panel or saddle flap and are usually designed to carry a short or Lonsdale girth. The more traditional saddles have two flaps, which can provide additional security when worn with an overgirth for the cross-country phase.

CROSS-COUNTRY JUMPS

To make the jumping of the cross-country phase a safe and positive experience, the horse and rider combination should be comfortable jumping a range of fence types at home and in a cross-country schooling situation before competing. Many competition centres offer simulated cross-country training days which provide the opportunity to jump portable cross-country fences, usually on a prepared surface, before the competitive season starts. Training such

as 'Jumping and Style' (JAS) classes allow the rider to develop the feel of riding in a forward rhythm over simulated cross-country fences, and provide them with feedback on their performance as a training activity. These days should not replace cross-country schooling but should be considered as a training activity where advice can be sought and the rider can assess their performance and skills before going cross-country schooling.

Horse and rider need to be comfortable jumping simple uprights and oxers as for normal show-jump training, but in addition, skills need to be developed to jump specialist fences such as steps, banks, drops, water, 'skinnies' (narrow fences), corners, and fences on related distances or curved lines. Many of these can be introduced by riding in a cross-country schooling field that has a variety of training fences at various heights with all-weather take-offs and landings. When the confidence and skills of the horse and rider have been established in this schooling situation, then the next training session can be taken on a proper cross-country course so that the jumping can be combined with the demands of the changing terrain and varying ground conditions.

Different types of cross-country fence, and the best way to ride them, are discussed below.

Uprights

An upright fence needs to be treated with considerable respect and should be jumped from a balanced and even pace. The horse needs time to see the design of the fence and to adjust his balance too, so the pace should be steadied to allow him to stay in rhythm, engage his hocks underneath himself, and then get his shoulders up and over the obstacle cleanly. The rider should be sitting with their shoulders upright, maintaining the horse's rhythm and 'waiting

THE IMPORTANCE OF THE CANTER

The canter, as for the show-jumping phase, is critical to the development of the horse's fitness and skill in jumping solid fences. In training the rider should work with different lengths of canter stride to establish the ability to lengthen and shorten the stride without losing any quality and balance within the pace.

In Fig. 5.4 the rider has allowed the horse to canter down the hill in good balance. She has kept

her upper body up, and both horse and rider are focused on the fence ahead of them. The horse has raised her head to look at the jump ahead without any restriction from the rider's contact.

In Fig. 5.5 as horse and rider approach the take-off point both are looking up, and the mare has the freedom to raise her head and neck, which is needed for a balanced take-off. The hind legs are coming forward to take the weight and push off the ground. The left fore will be the last leg to leave the ground as the mare actually takes off to jump. The rider has her weight in the foot (although more would be preferred for a totally independent position), and is sitting straight and balanced; ideally she could be a little taller so as not to potentially come in front of the movement at the point of take-off.

ABOVE: *Fig. 5.4 Good canter on approach to a fence.*

RIGHT: Fig. 5.5 *Good canter for take-off.*

Fig. 5.6 An inexperienced horse jumping an upright.

for the fence to come to them', rather than allowing the stride to lengthen and the pace to accelerate.

Figs 5.6 and 5.7 show the same upright fence jumped by two different horses, each with their own individual style. The horse in Fig 5.6 is young and inexperienced, throwing a rather awkward jump over a small upright; the rider has taken a secure position over the fence allowing the horse to jump freely forward. Both horse and rider are straight, and both show good balance. In time a better bascule over the horse's back would be desirable.

In Fig. 5.7 the same fence is jumped by a more confident horse, which has approached the fence from a strong canter: this has made the rider defensive in her position and rather strong in the hand (note the open mouth). She needs to develop greater security in her lower leg to produce a more independent position.

Spreads

A spread fence can be ridden out of a more forward stride. The design of the fence allows the horse to assess the fence and jump from a stronger rhythm; roll tops and brush fences are particularly inviting types of spread. However, note that hayracks and pheasant feeders can present a false ground line, so care should be taken, particularly at different times of the day where shadows can influence the take-off line.

Banks/Steps

Jumping up a bank or steps should be treated in the same way as jumping an upright: it needs a balanced approach with the horse on his hocks – ideally the horse should take off close to the bank face as opposed to standing off. This allows for a clean jump up, with plenty of energy when the horse is on the step or bank to continue moving forwards. The rider should maintain their weight in the stirrup and off the horse's

*Fig. 5.7
Strong
horse
jumping
an upright.*

Fig. 5.8 An inexperienced horse coming down steps.

Fig. 5.9 A good jump down steps.

back to allow him to keep the power in the hindquarters. When going down steps, the rider needs to have their weight a little behind the vertical, keeping the centre of balance behind the horse's withers. The weight should be in the heel, with the lower leg coming a little in front of the vertical; the rider's leg needs to stay on the horse in case he should hesitate coming off the step. At all times the rider should be looking up and away to the next fence or their exit line.

Figs 5.8 and 5.9 show the young, inexperienced horse tackling her first drop fence: the rider has approached the step in a forward trot allowing the horse the freedom to look and assess the situation. She has remained straight on the top of the bank and is balanced in her position. The mare has taken the weight on to her hind legs well, but has been rather cautious in stepping down. The rider is quiet but confident, and is riding her positively forwards, but without rushing her.

After a couple of approaches down the steps, the young horse has developed more confidence in both the situation and the rider, and in Fig. 5.9 she is confidently cantering off the step, with the rider allowing her the freedom to do so.

Figs 5.10 and 5.11 show the more educated

Fig. 5.10 Jumping up steps.

Fig 5.11   Landing up steps.

horse throwing a good, impulsive jump up on to the first step: the approach is uphill and so the canter needs plenty of energy without excessive speed. The rider has her weight securely in the foot, her contact allowing the horse to go forwards and her weight just off his back, allowing him to use his hind legs efficiently.

In Fig. 5.11 the horse has pushed off the first step with energy and is looking confident. The rider has followed the movement of the horse but is still keeping her weight through to the foot. Her next responsibility will be to re-establish the quality of the canter as she rides away from the steps.

Drops

The height of the drop, or the steps down,

will dictate the appropriate pace to approach the fence. The landing will also influence the speed, and the rider will need to assess whether the ground is level or sloping away. Another consideration is the proximity of the next fence after the drop/steps, as this will give you more or less time to recover a weak position. It is sensible to approach in a forward-thinking pace, not too fast but allowing the horse to be off the forehand; it is better to come in a forward-thinking trot than a backward canter. If the rider approaches too quickly, it is easy to lose the security of the lower leg, particularly on landing, and then be tipped forwards and so out of balance.

A drop fence should always be approached from a straight line. Avoid angles, as a twist from the horse if he leaves a leg behind is very likely to send the rider out of the side door. If the horse jumps rather large then the rider should slip the reins to avoid restricting the neck and the horse's balance; this is particularly important if jumping into water. Slipping the reins involves the rider leaning slightly back and opening the fingers to allow the rein to slide through the hand. This skill should be practised at home over simple fences so that on the course this technique can be used when and if needed.

Water

The test of jumping into water is actually asking the horse to get his feet wet, rather than how deep the water is. At the lower levels, the entry point into the water is generally no more than a slope running into the water itself, which enables the horse to assess the water from a distance. As he gains in confidence he will be progressing up the competition levels and the 'questions' will get progressively harder: he may be asked to jump into the water from a step, then perhaps to jump a fence before the water, so he lands on solid ground before entering the water itself, and eventually to jump a fence into water; as his education and experience increase there may be a fence actually in the water.

Whatever the question, water will have a drag effect on the horse's forward momentum, and the deeper the water the harder it is for him to lift his front legs forward for the next stride. If your horse is cautious and maybe a little spooky then he will need to be ridden more strongly to encourage him; if he is confident and inclined to jump boldly into the water, then a more cautious approach is advised. Either way, let him find his balance on landing and allow him to travel forward to the exit; a trot is better if there is a step out of the water as this produces less water spray, making it easier for the horse to see the obstacle out of the water.

Ditches

Ditches often concern the rider more than the horse and should be approached confidently and positively, with the rider looking up and forwards to the next fence. The horse is a naturally cautious animal, so he may find a hole in the ground rather alarming the first time he meets one; it is therefore a good idea to introduce ditches early on in the horse's cross-country training.

Ditches need to be approached from a lengthening stride with plenty of impulsion to keep the horse thinking forwards. Providing the ditch has a good ground line they usually help the horse judge where to take off. The easiest ditch fence is often where the ditch is in front of a fence such as a palisade or hedge: this type of fence sometimes looks quite daunting but it usually rides very well as the ditch acts as a take-off point and prevents the horse from getting too close to the fence.

Other types of fence incorporating a ditch are the trakehner, where the ditch is underneath a fence such as a log or rails, or in a combination such as hollows. A ditch on the landing side of a fence rarely causes the horse any concern as his natural jump should easily clear it before he even sees it.

Fig. 5.12 shows a novice horse tackling her first ditch: she is showing a healthy respect for the hole in the ground, though the dropped pole gives her something to focus on, rather than the ditch itself. She had previously jumped over the ditch without the pole. She is straight, but is overjumping due to her lack of experience. The rider has a secure position, a good lower leg and is looking forwards, though she could allow the horse a little more freedom in the neck over the fence.

In Fig. 5.13 horse and rider are looking very comfortable. The horse is more experienced and has measured the demands of the fence, and has jumped conservatively. The rider is straight and in good balance,

Fig. 5.12   Introducing a young horse to a ditch.

although could have more weight through the lower leg.

Hollows

This type of fence should be approached in a strong show-jumping canter with plenty of engagement and impulsion. This allows the horse time to look, adjust his weight, and then jump confidently through the fence, ditch, fence combination. Most riders do not address the quality of the canter early enough and the horse is left trying to find his balance on the last stride to the fence, which often leads to a refusal or an awkward jump. The canter should be contained in sufficient time so the first element of the combination can be approached in a forward rhythm in the last few strides, with the horse on the aids, listening and responsive to the rider. The rider should be sitting up with their shoulders upright waiting for the first fence to come to them, rather than pushing forwards to meet it: this is particularly important if the first element is an upright.

Fig. 5.13   *A more experienced horse jumping a ditch confidently.*

Corners

The corner fence is seen at almost every level of competition and should be treated with respect. It demands control and accuracy to jump well, and the rider must be sure to hold their line all the way to the fence so the horse is forward thinking. Ideally a strong show-jumping canter is the most suitable pace, particularly when learning how to hold a line to the jump. The safest and most accurate way to find the best line to jump a corner is to dissect it from its point through to the widest part; this then presents a vertical face, which may be approached in the same way as an upright.

Some corners are filled in whilst others are more open in their construction, but both demand respect, although the filled-in version is safer for the less experienced combination if the horse tries to bank it or drifts towards the wider part.

Figs 5.14–5.16 show how a simple fence can be constructed in the school to educate both horse and rider in jumping corners. Initially the fence should be small, with a clear groundline, as can be seen in Fig. 5.14. The rider has approached from canter, and

TOP AND MIDDLE: **Figs. 5.14 and 5.15 Schooling for jumping corners.**

Fig. 5.16   Schooling for jumping bigger corners.

the horse has stood off the fence slightly: his hind legs are not a pair as he jumps, although he is starting to make a good shape as he takes off.

In Fig. 5.15 the horse is showing a nice shape over the fence. The rider is in balance with a secure lower leg, and is allowing the horse the freedom to jump confidently. Note that at this point the corner is relatively narrow, allowing the rider to jump straight through the middle of the corner. Once confidence in holding a line has been established, the corner can be made progressively wider and higher, in line with the requirements at each level of eventing.

In Fig. 5.16 the rider has approached just right of the centre: horse and rider are straight, and showing good posture and balance. Note the introduction of flags in the schooling session at home, as this helps both horse and rider stay focused on their line.

Skinnies and Arrowheads

Narrow fences are all about straightness and the line to the jump. The rider needs to have control of the pace and line, and must not be too quick, as this can lead to a run-out on the last stride. Keep the canter contained without allowing the stride to lengthen, with plenty of impulsion but still riding forwards. The rider needs to be focused on where they are going, looking ahead to the next fence and their getaway.

Figs 5.17–5.19 demonstrate the steps involved in educating a horse and rider in jumping narrow fences: the exercise is not intended to 'dare' either party. Skinnies and technical fences should be introduced at home in the school where they can be constructed to support the learning and confidence of the horse and rider. There is no harm in quietly showing the horse the newly constructed fence before asking him to jump it.

Once the horse is confident about jumping the skinny – in this case half a filler – with the guide poles raised, they can be dropped to the floor so they continue to help channel the horse over the fence. If possible flags on either side of the fence can be used to support the straightness and help as a visual reference for both horse and rider.

By developing the exercises from the basics and establishing the horse's straightness and confidence at each level, he will learn what the question is, and will jump confidently through and over a narrow fence. In Fig. 5.19 the horse and rider are straight and appear confident without the use of guide poles.

CROSS-COUNTRY EXERCISES

Many of the skills needed for jumping across the country can be developed at home in the arena. This is known as 'simulated cross-country', and there are often specific training days organized through British Eventing, and local competition/training centres that offer this opportunity. By practising such skills in an arena the rider can learn about lines, turns and establishing an independent position before going out on to the undulating terrain of a cross-country course. Training over simulated fences and lines is not an excuse for not going cross-country schooling: think of it as a warm-up and a learning opportunity.

The following exercises are a suggestion of some training exercises that would improve the skills and confidence of any horse working up to and including British Eventing Novice level. These skills should be built on from those established during the show-jumping training, and should be developed with the rider working at their cross-country stirrup length whether the training takes place in an arena or a field.

Fig. 5.17   Introducing a skinny.

Exercise 1: Two/Three/ Four Bounces from Trot

This exercise is a good way to focus on the correct technique for the horse; it also encourages him to look for the fence because there are no ground poles acting as groundlines.

The aims of the exercise are as follows:

● To develop the horse's technique and athleticism or gymnastic ability without having to jump a big fence.

● To establish the rhythm and consistency of pace.
● To improve the suppleness of both horse and rider.
● To allow the rider to be responsible for their own balance and control, independent of the horse.

The exercise may be developed as follows:

● An initial place pole is set down 2.7m (9ft) from the first raised upright of about 75cm (2ft 6in). The rider approaches in rising

TOP: **Fig. 5.18   Establishing straightness.**

LEFT: **Fig. 5.19   Establishing confidence.**

trot, asking for canter at the place pole. The horse should quietly take canter and jump over the small upright.

● As the horse understands the exercise, additional uprights of 75cm can be added until there is a series of two, three or four fences each at a bounce distance of 3.3–3.6m (11–12ft). On landing over the last fence the horse should remain in an engaged canter: it is important to ride away in canter so that the horse stays forward thinking and in front of the rider's leg.

The exercise should be repeated from both reins. If the rider approaches from the left rein then they should ride away to the right, returning to approach from the right; then progress through the exercise again, but ride away to the left.

Although single raised poles are used here, the exercise can be modified with high cross poles as a variation during training; this will encourage the horse to remain straight if there is a tendency for him to drift. As with the initial exercise, not having groundlines

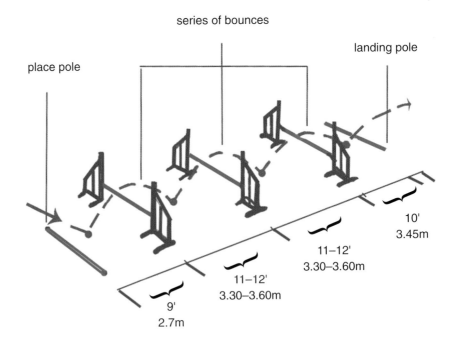

Fig. 5.20 Cross-country bounce exercise.

encourages a softer bascule, allowing the horse to develop a more athletic technique over the fence.

To increase the difficulty of the exercise, a single fence can be added, placed 5.5m (18ft) after the last bounce. This will encourage the horse to wait for the fence whilst maintaining the quality of the canter from the impulsion generated by the bounces.

The rider's responsibility is as follows:

- To maintain their independent position and balance through the exercise. The weight should remain in the stirrup, thereby developing a secure lower leg position and avoiding leaning forward on to the horse's shoulders. The rider needs to follow the movement of the horse's neck with a yielding hand and arm.
- To allow the horse the freedom and independence to jump and maintain his balance, bascule and rhythm throughout the exercise.
- To ride away from the exercise in an engaged canter, created by the impulsion from the bounces.
- To re-establish the working trot through a good quality transition, and allow repetition of the exercise.

Problem Solving

- **Rushing.**
  If the horse is inclined to quicken through the exercise, then the trot can be maintained over the initial place pole and the distance reduced to 2.4m (8ft). If the horse is finding the exercise easy and is becoming complacent, then another bounce fence can be used (and so on up to five), and the technical difficulty increased by finishing the exercise with a single fence from one stride – 5.5m (18ft) – away. This will make the horse

respect the exercise, and teach him to wait for the last element to come to him.
- **Lack of straightness.**
  Not being straight can be due to the horse favouring his weaker side, but more often is caused by the rider losing straightness, either by having more weight in one stirrup, or by twisting the upper body. If this problem persists and the horse is drifting one way, then poles can be placed on the ground between the bounces on the side the horse is consistently drifting towards: this will encourage him to stay true to the line that he should be jumping on. Using cross poles instead of uprights may help both horse and rider develop better straightness.
- **Poor bascule.**
  It is important that the rider is independent in their position and not losing balance on to the horse's shoulders. Check by consciously 'stepping' into the stirrup at the point of take-off to maintain the security of the lower leg.

Exercise 2: Jumping a Fence on Different Lines

The aims of the exercise are as follows:

- To develop straightness and forward riding whilst maintaining a regular stride.
- To develop the ability for the rider to ride forwards.
- To hold a line to and away from a single fence.
- To jump a fence in a specific place.

The exercise may be developed as follows:

- Make sure that your horse is suitably warmed up on the flat, and then warm up over a small upright to begin with.

Fig. 5.21   *Jumping in the centre of the fence.*

- Pay particular attention to the quality of the canter.
- It helps if the fence has a good groundline and is constructed with poles of alternating colours; this way the rider can aim for a particular section of the pole, and is able to assess their straightness.
- Once the exercise is established, the upright can be made into a small (low and wide) oxer. Be aware that when jumping an oxer across the diagonal this will increase the width of the spread and produce a much larger jump (bascule) over the fence.
- These skills should be developed and established before moving on to Exercise 3.

Figs 5.21–5.23 show how this exercise may be used to develop accuracy and straightness when jumping a fence. In Fig. 5.21 the horse is showing a good shape and position over the centre of the fence.

Fig. 5.22   Jumping left of centre.

In Fig. 5.22 he is jumping just to the left of centre – ideally this could be a little more over the white section of the pole, but most important is the fact that horse and rider are straight.

Fig. 5.23 is a much better example of jumping to the right of centre, where the horse is clearly positioned over the white section of the pole, and horse and rider are focused on the landing and the direction of travel.

Once straightness has been established when approaching the fence on a straight line, the rider can put this to the test by jumping the fence at an angle, when it is even more important to stay straight and true to your line (Fig. 5.23).

The rider's responsibility is as follows:

- To maintain an independent position to, over and away from the fences.
- To learn to see and ride to a straight

Fig. 5.23   Jumping diagonally across the fence.

line from a distance, and to stay on the line.

● To learn to hold the horse on the line through their position, and most importantly through the leg.

Problem Solving

● **Drifting off line.**
The rider must first be able to jump a small upright approaching from a straight line so that they meet the centre of the fence. Until this is achieved the exercise cannot progress correctly. If the rider is struggling to see the line as they approach the fence, then guide poles can be placed on the approach to, and on the landing side of, the fence. These need to be wide enough for the horse to pass through comfortably, and should be placed about three strides before and after the upright.

● **Drifting or bulging out over the fence.**
Some horses lack straightness over a fence and will consistently drift to the left or the right. The horse should be assessed if he is doing this regularly, whichever canter lead the fence is approached on. In such cases there may be an issue with the quality of the canter, and the horse's ability to push off equally with both hind limbs on take-off, which causes him to drift. Check that he is pushing off equally and is balanced on take-off: if he is not, then the canter is the issue and not the jump, and it is a flatwork concern.

If the horse is always drifting but is taking off equally, then the rider's straightness should be assessed. A rider will often have a stronger or weaker side, and this will show up at the point of take-off because if the rider twists or leans one way, the thrust of their weight through the stirrups will be greater on that side. The rider's positional straightness therefore needs to be addressed before the exercise can continue correctly. This may also show up as the horse always landing on one particular canter lead due to the change in the rider's weight/position.

Exercise 3: Riding Lines and Angles

The aims of the exercise are as follows:

● To develop straightness and forward riding whilst maintaining a regular stride and rhythm between the fences.
● To develop the rider's ability to ride forwards.
● To increase suppleness and obedience in the horse.

With reference to Fig. 5.24, the exercise may be developed as follows:

● Initially the centre fence needs to be built in a suitable arena or field allowing plenty of room to set up the two uprights and two oxers on diagonal lines and at standard distances from each other.
● The height is not important and the fences need to be simple enough not to be problematic for the horse or rider. Each of the fences should be built so it can be jumped safely from either direction.
● Warm up initially over a small upright and then one of the oxers; this will allow you and your horse to be confident jumping the actual fences.
● Start jumping through the two straight lines from oxer to upright and back again. Focus on the quality of the strides and the regularity of the pace. When the set number of strides is achieved, then the line can be jumped on the diagonal of uprights with the focus being exactly the same. When this is established the diagonal line of oxers can be introduced.

The rider's responsibility is as follows:

● To develop and maintain the horse and rider focus between fences, staying on the line and riding to the set number of strides as built.
● To maintain an independent position to, over and away from the fences.
● To learn to see and ride to a straight line from a distance, and to stay on the line.

The rider can count the number of strides between the fences as the horse will always jump on a whole number. By doing this, the rider starts to develop a feel for the rhythm and the pace.

Problem Solving
● **Drifting off line.**
Make sure that the canter is being ridden forwards but still in a good rhythm;

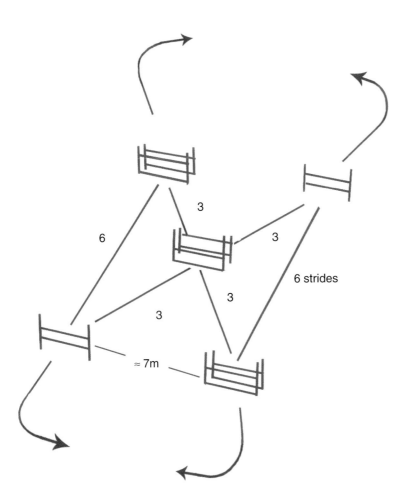

Fig. 5.24   Riding lines and angles.

return to the middle oxer on its own to establish the regularity of the stride to and away from the fence. Once straightness over the single fence has been established, then progress through the exercise as before. The rider needs to consider their own straightness, particularly over the fence. Too strong a

contact in one hand can cause the horse to deviate off line.

● **Over-jumping.**
Over-jumping often happens at oxers when the horse is presented to the fence without enough impulsion in the canter. The horse arrives at the fence take-off point in a poor pace, making

it difficult for him to make a smooth and even bascule. This is even more critical on the cross-country phase, but applies in principle to all aspects of jumping. At best the horse produces an awkward jump or refuses. The quality of the canter needs to be addressed by the rider in order to maintain a positive approach. It is best to go back a step and re-establish the canter strides between the two straight related fences on the six strides before returning to the diagonal lines.

Exercise 4: Curved Lines

Many of the combinations on cross-country courses now offer the rider the choice of riding a safer but longer route, or the opportunity to ride a straighter line between fences but where the actual fences must be jumped on the diagonal.

The aims of the exercise are as follows:

- For the rider to maintain the rhythm, and establish control of the pace and the line chosen through a line of fences with a change of direction.
- To improve the suppleness of the horse.
- To develop co-ordination of the rider's aids and balance as well as their ability to ride forward to the next fence.

The exercise may be developed as follows:

- Warm up the horse well on the flat and over a few small uprights. The fences do not have to be very high as the exercise concerns the lines rather than the fence heights.
- Initially approach the first fence in a balanced canter, land and ride a curved line to the centre fence on an even number of strides (four). On landing continue to turn the same way as the approach. Once this has been established the third fence with the change of direction can be added.
- Approach fence one on the same regular canter, and jump the centre fence in the middle of the jump; at the point of take-off the rider should focus on landing and riding a curved line to the third fence on the other rein. This should be repeated until an even number of strides can be ridden on a regular curve.
- The exercise can then be developed by approaching fence one in the same regular canter, but riding a straight line through the middle of the centre fence (on three strides) and then on to the third fence (on three strides), whilst still maintaining a straight line.
- Once established the exercise can be reversed so that the approach can be made from the other rein, thus developing the suppleness and athleticism of the horse on both reins.

The rider's responsibility is as follows:

- To make decisions and stay with them whether jumping the curved or the straight line.
- The rider needs to be independent of the horse and in balance, clearly indicating at the point of take-off what their intentions are: either to jump the curved line or take the diagonal line.
- When jumping the curved line the rider needs to keep their weight through to the inside stirrup, and adjust to the new inside line over the centre fence, at the same time opening the inside rein to enforce a positive change in the direction. The centre fence should always be jumped from a straight approach.
- To keep their centre of gravity central to the horse, staying in balance and avoiding coming in front of the movement.

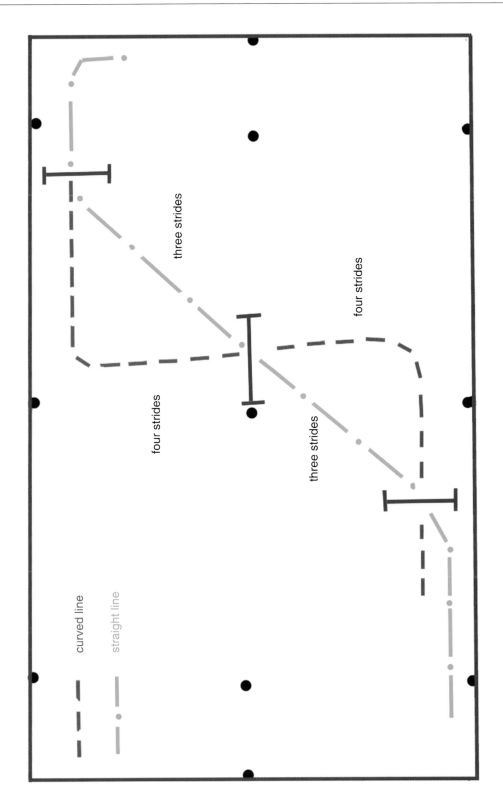

Fig. 5.25   Curved lines.

Problem Solving

- **Wrong canter lead.**
  As the rider approaches the fence they need to be quite clear about which direction they wish to turn or travel in. They need to step into their inside stirrup to allow the horse to follow their weight and take the correct lead. The rider also has to consider the quality of the canter on the approach to allow the horse to jump well with good balance and bascule over the fence, allowing the horse the freedom of his back to land and move forward in balance on the correct lead.

- **Lack of straightness.**
  The rider needs to focus on riding positively on a forward stride with the canter covering a suitable distance to jump through the exercise on an even number of strides. The rider should consider how they are sitting and what their body is communicating to the horse. They need to be straight with their contact, clearly indicating the directions of travel that the horse should be taking.

- **Running out.**
  Make sure that the fences are small enough not to be an issue for the horse or the rider. Check that the line is not too tight, and that the horse is approaching the fence from a forward balanced canter. Readjust the line and if necessary take a step back and establish the balance to the fence on the curved lines before progressing to the straight diagonal ones.

6 Psychological Considerations for the Rider

SPORT PSYCHOLOGY

In the broadest sense of the terminology 'sport psychology' is the ability to approach an achievement situation with the confidence and the knowledge that both body and mind are prepared for optimal performance. Sport psychology encompasses the psychological aspects of competitive sport, exercise, fitness, leisure and motor skill development. Many riders do not perceive themselves as athletes – even though they are happy to see their horse as athletic, and as such give the horse the athletic considerations that will enhance its performance. There are, however, many aspects of the human mind that need consideration and development to allow us, as riders, to be well prepared for competitions, confident in our ability to achieve, and consciously aware of the strengths and weaknesses within our performance. This allows us to reflect positively and to improve over time, with training, and through competition experience.

The achievement of goals, development of confidence and the ability to manage our anxieties are all-important psychological considerations that do need consideration within our own personal training plan. These factors affect everything the performer does, which in turn either directly or indirectly influences the degree to which the athlete achieves the task-specific ideal performance state.

Psychological Skills: Mental Imagery

Riders are very good at using mental imagery relating to their horse's performance. Sometimes this is a positive skill – for instance, many riders can visualize themselves riding through a dressage test. In Fig. 6.1 the rider is approaching her halt: the horse is a little flexed to the left, but the rider is straight and the horse is straight on the line of travel. The rider is showing a positive attitude: a smile costs nothing, and a dressage judge is a real person and not someone to be frightened of.

In Fig. 6.2, by being positive on their approach to the halt, horse and rider are perfectly straight and square. This is a good halt, and the rider should remember this feeling and visualize the approach, the straightness and the achievement in order to produce the same result in the future.

Mental imagery can equally be a negative skill if the rider applies it to a previous performance and creates similar expectations for their horse's behaviour. Typically this can be seen if a rider expects a horse to shy at something: probably it will, not necessarily because it is spooked, but because the rider's body language and expectations have conditioned it to respond in such a way to the external stimulus.

Positive images should be created using the imagination in definite ways in order to create inspirational and positive visions, target goals, and prepare yourself to follow the game plan. The rider should visualize their performance in high definition colour and sound. When

Fig. 6.1 Riding forwards towards halt on the centre line.

jumping, practise visualizing the fence in front of you, vivid in its colours and design. Image the feel of the horse and the sounds of the hoofbeats as you approach the fence, being aware of your perfect approach around the corner to the line that you want to take, sensing the response to the horse as he takes off over the fence – being aware of your body as you move in balance over the fence as the horse successfully jumps the jump and starts to land. You are looking ahead to the next fence as the horse completes the jump cleanly and moves on to the next fence on the course.

If a rider has negative thoughts about an aspect of the competition, then the same skills apply. For instance, if they are worried about people watching the dressage test, then before the test begins they should learn to focus solely on the test that they need to ride. As they visualize the environment, the judge's box or car should be seen as grey and insignificant, and the area outside the arena should be faded out so that, while the rider can clearly see the arena boards and the dressage letters and can practise visualizing riding through the test in the arena, they avoid any external distractions. Learning this skill develops clear visualizing techniques; it also supports the rider's ability to focus internally and externally, selecting what

Fig. 6.2 Establishing halt on the centre line.

they need to be aware of depending upon the situation and the external distractions.

Imagery may therefore be considered as a positive skill: it gives the ability to visualize certain situations, such as positively visualizing a clear round across country, or negatively believing that your horse will stop at the ditch. Equally it gives the ability to associate a feeling with behaviour. For example, if a horse is anxious – as in Fig. 6.3 he may be nervous about a situation, or perhaps he is being poorly ridden – the rider might assume that this feeling will happen every time the event is repeated. However, the rider needs to become more aware of the cause of the incident in an objective way, and then to positively associate it with a good feeling when they achieve a good result.

In Fig. 6.4 the rider is happy and relaxed as the horse jumps the ditch, demonstrating the association between positive feelings and a successful outcome. If the rider is worried about a particular type of fence but always associates it with ease of jumping, then they will approach it every time with positive energy and a positive expectation. By using positive imagery – what the approach looks

ABOVE: **Fig. 6.3   Negative feelings.**

BELOW: **Fig. 6.4   Positive feelings.**

Fig. 6.5   Visualization.

like, how it feels to jump the fence, and what it looks like to ride away – then this will always be a positive experience.

Mental skills need training in order to build up a performance, but as we have seen, riders are generally good at this – for example, mentally riding a show-jumping round before even getting on the horse, or learning a dressage test by visualizing themselves riding their own horse, starting from riding down the centre line towards the judge at C, and then continuing through the test in the same manner.

Stressful Situations

Riders need to be able to cope with all types of stressful situations, such as injury, travel, the weather, but in order to do this they need to have considered the likelihood of these situations occurring, and have an action plan to cope. Events tend to fall into two categories: those you can control, and those that you can't. It is beyond anyone's ability to control the weather, but we can put strategies in place for dealing with the probability of poor conditions,

and consequently can be in control of making the decisions to deal with the situation.

With such skills available for the rider they can be better prepared and develop mental readiness. This allows a person to take advantage of performance opportunities, to develop essential mental and physical skills, and as a consequence reflect effectively and objectively. Riders must also be able to focus on different aspects of the competition situation. It is important to know where riders are in the collecting ring, but not to the point that you cannot ride around them: this is known as 'distraction control'. Distraction control develops skills for controlling distractions (other riders), maintaining a positive and effective focus (environmental situations), regaining an effective focus, and being able to keep to your own working-in plan. The development of these skills allows the rider to be fully focused on the job in hand; some athletes would call it being 'in the zone', but either way it allows the rider to be released from anything else that is irrelevant at that time. Confidence can rise or fall depending on the quality of experience and the extent to which you can develop mental strength.

It is very easy for a rider to overreact when a horse has a sharp or naughty moment. If the situation is perceived as stressful, then the rider will begin to expect the horse to behave in a similar manner. But horses are not human, and as such do not react to the same things that we do – but they do pick up on our behaviour. If our body language suggests that the horse may misbehave and we are tense, then he is likely to pick up the rider tension and as a consequence not be on the aids and potentially misbehave – thus fulfilling the rider's feelings that they had something to be anxious about!

However, by the rider believing in their own behaviour and riding skills, they can put the horse back on the aids and restore confidence in each other. So the horse can be fresh and overreact to a situation, but then it is even

Fig. 6.6 Our tension may be transmitted to the horse and influence his behaviour.

more important that the rider is in a position of confidence and security to place the horse back into a position of relaxation and concentration.

The Competition Environment

The environment can have both a facilitative and debilitative effect upon the achievement of an ideal competitive state: the lorry park, collecting ring and scoreboards can be stressful environments if the rider allows them to be. Other aspects are concerned with the ability to organize, worrying about the quality of previous training, the motivational climate for the individual rider, the feeling of fatigue of overtraining, and lastly the social support that is available. Each of these factors can impact differently with individuals, but they should all be well thought out when considering how to manage and control potentially stressful environments.

It is quite normal to have periods of anxiety when competing, and a few nerves are probably a good thing. Often stress is referred to in a negative sense, but some stress actually produces an aroused mental and physical state that supports the motivation and energy to actually perform and achieve a positive outcome. Managing stress is the ability to understand and appraise the situation to develop coping strategies. Too much stress produces outward symptoms that are physical (somatic), psychological (cognitive) and behavioural (visual) – *see* panel opposite.

'Butterflies' are a prime example of a physical feeling about having nerves. This feeling is real and should be accepted by the rider. Through acceptance of the feeling the rider can learn to deal with it. It is not a question of getting rid of the butterflies, but more about understanding why they are there, and coping with them. Some people give these physical signs of anxiety a positive label, for instance the feeling of having butterflies can be changed from a negative perception by using self talk to suggest that this is a feeling of excitement and positive anticipation of the ensuing activity.

Fig. 6.7   Calm and relaxation established.

THE COMPETITION DAY

Before the Event

Competing should be about putting the training skills that have been developed out of the eventing season into practice. The competition environment is not the place to 'have a go' and see what happens – this attitude is likely to produce some surprise results and certainly some unpredicted outcomes, neither of which is desirable. In order to determine what it is realistic to aim for – and more importantly, what is achievable – the rider should start with some realistic goals. Goal setting is a valuable training tool to support a training plan and show progression, and by setting realistic targets the rider can see that they are being met and progress is being made.

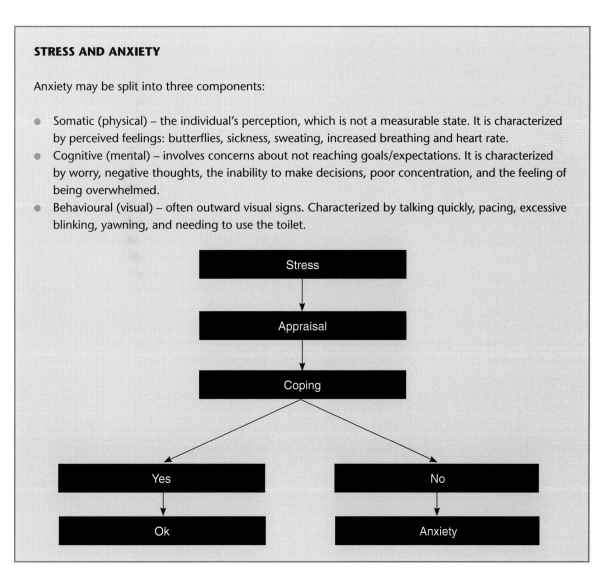

STRESS AND ANXIETY

Anxiety may be split into three components:

● Somatic (physical) – the individual's perception, which is not a measurable state. It is characterized by perceived feelings: butterflies, sickness, sweating, increased breathing and heart rate.
● Cognitive (mental) – involves concerns about not reaching goals/expectations. It is characterized by worry, negative thoughts, the inability to make decisions, poor concentration, and the feeling of being overwhelmed.
● Behavioural (visual) – often outward visual signs. Characterized by talking quickly, pacing, excessive blinking, yawning, and needing to use the toilet.

Stress

Appraisal

Coping

Yes

No

Ok

Anxiety

Fig. 6.8   Stress and anxiety flow chart.

The Event Itself

The first place where anxieties can potentially creep in is in the lorry park. As the time gets closer to performing the dressage test, nerves can start to develop and influence the behaviour of the rider, and consequently the way in which the horse will be able to perform. Before getting ready for the dressage phase the rider should find somewhere quiet to reflect on the test itself: they should ride the test in their mind, feeling and reflecting upon the way that they prepare for each of the movements, the transitions, and the way they expect their horse to go. Riders are very good at this, as they often visualize the test as if riding it with the horse's ears in front of them.

The rider should be realistic in their expectations of the test performance, since by now they should know what they and their horse are naturally good at. If the canter work is the best pace, then this may be a more suitable pace to ride in around the arena before the judge gives the signal that they can start. If transitions are the best way of keeping the horse listening and making him pay attention in the test, then these can be ridden around the outside of the arena before the bell is rung to begin the test.

If the rider is realistic about their ability to perform then they can focus on the areas that need support and attention. Remember that the horse will only be as good as the rider asking him to work: too often riders get inside the arena and freeze, expecting the horse to know what to do – but the horse needs to be informed of what is going to happen next, he hasn't learnt the test! If he loses balance or concentration around a corner or through a transition, then it is the rider's responsibility to support him through rebalancing the work and focusing on the next movement. All these considerations should be run through as a mental dress rehearsal, the rider focusing on what is likely to happen and how they can appraise the situation to cope and produce a good test.

The Dressage Test

Once a mental dress rehearsal has been completed, then the horse can be tacked up and the rider can get on and make their way to the dressage arenas. The warm-up area is often busy and crowded and can be an intimidating place to ride in if the rider loses focus on what they wish to achieve at this point. Try to avoid just drifting around, but instead find a quiet space and focus on settling the horse on your aids: this is the prime purpose of working in. This should take about twenty minutes or so depending upon the individual horse and the weather conditions (in cold weather the horse will need more time to warm up and loosen up). When the horse before you has been called up from the warm-up area, quietly go through your plan of what you need to do in these last few minutes (remove the horse's boots, put on your jacket, and so on).

When you are called forward to the arena, be positive and ride purposefully towards the judge: a cheerful greeting stating your name and number helps the writer confirm who you are. Ride confidently around the arena in the direction and pace that you have pre-planned. When the judge rings their bell for you to start, quietly proceed to the 'A' end of the arena. A quiet word to your horse or a pat can put your nerves at ease. Remember to ride positively through the A end of the arena down the centre line with your body language stating that you have as much right to be here as anyone else and this is going to be a good test. Look directly at the judge's car in order to make a positive first statement for your entrance.

Ride the whole test as if you are riding at home, and don't be afraid to make corrections to the horse's way of going. Support him by riding him in balance and clearly stating through your body language what he must do next. Use sitting trot to support the upward and downward transitions. Be positive and ride him forwards: he will then be much straighter, more connected and forward thinking throughout, and you are then being actively responsible for his way of going. If an error occurs in the test, quietly correct it if you can, otherwise just continue: mistakes do happen but they don't need to influence the whole performance.

At the end of the test, turn down the centre line and ride as purposefully as you did for your entrance. The horse's level of education will determine how you ride the transition to halt for your final salute: a few steps of sitting trot to balance him through the transition is recommended, and two to three steps of walk before halting is permitted in the lower level tests; however, higher marks will be awarded for a clean transition to halt. Remember to ride the halt, quietly correcting the horse if he steps out of line, reinforcing the aids until he is still and settled. A confident salute to the judge finishes your test, and a pat to your horse never goes amiss. Quietly leave the arena and return to the lorry park.

The Jumping Phases

The same mental preparation should repeat itself for both the show-jumping and the cross-country phases. The rider should quietly reflect on the needs of each section before leaving the lorry park and making their way to the collecting ring. The course should be ridden in the rider's mind, considering the lines, turns and the approach and exit to each of the fences. Once an obstacle has been jumped, the focus should move to the next one, whatever happened at the previous fence.

The rider's individual personality will determine whether or not they visit the scoreboard and check their scores between phases: for some, knowing how they are doing can be a positive boost for their confidence, while for others it has a negative effect because they see the other competitors' scores and start competing against these, often putting extra pressure on themselves to perform better.

Post Event

After the cross-country is the time to reflect on the day's performance and outcome. It is human nature to run through the event and think about 'what if' scenarios, but this is often not very realistic and frequently does not reflect the true performance. A successful outcome is naturally a boost to confidence, and it is quite acceptable to enjoy the winning feeling at the end of the day; it is also quite normal to be despondent if things did not work out as planned. Either way it is sensible to actively choose to reflect on your competitive performance on the following day, when the event is still fresh in your mind and you can be more objective about your performance in each of the sections. It is important to reflect on the competition in order to address the various aspects of any goals that have been set: depending upon the outcome of the event the goals can be ticked off as achieved, or revisited and adjusted if required.

It is also important to develop a positive attitude of self reflection so that achievements may be assessed and goals adjusted if necessary. Only by considering the psychological aspects of the rider's performance and achievements can steady, realistic progression be made and sustained.

PLANNING AND GOAL SETTING

Goals are something we are trying to achieve and are vitally important if motivation and self-confidence are to be sustained or increased. Goals fall into three categories: short, medium and long term. They help the rider aspire to achieving a realistic outcome, so they need to have a specific focus, such as jumping clear round a certain height or class. Goals set should have a degree of difficulty: if they are too easy no real effort need be put into achieving the result, and the sense of achievement and progress does not occur. Since working with horses is by definition unpredictable it is also advisable that any goals are flexible: horses are not reliable like machines, and may upset any pre-planning by losing a shoe, refusing to load, being off-colour. As riders we understand and deal with setbacks very well (events cancelled, lorry not starting, work commitments), learning to reorganize goals and our plans. Winning élite riders do not achieve their success by luck: they have actively and progressively planned their route, both for themselves and for their horses.

The goals set may be summarized by the acronym 'SMARTER', as follows:

Specific	Competing in a Novice dressage (BD) competition
Measurable	Gaining over 63 per cent as a test result
Achievable	Horse and rider combination have the necessary test skills
Realistic	Achieving 68 per cent in a Prelim test, so step up to Novice is realistic
Time based	To be aimed at in January before the new event season
Exciting	Challenging to compete under some pressure
Recordable	Able to record test result for future reference

THE BENEFITS OF GOAL SETTING

Why should we set goals and plan to achieve them? Achieving goals helps the rider to improve their performance through 'ticking off' their achievements. Working hard at home with a goal in mind will improve the quality of the practice and training sessions. Goals help to clarify our expectations as a rider as to what we want to do, and the route that the training and work will take us down. This is especially important when learning a new task, as the initial period of understanding and skill acquisition can be frustrating whilst the skill and task are learnt. From achieving this progression the rider will increase their intrinsic motivation, which is their reason for wanting to work hard and improve. The consequence to this developmental process is that it will increase rider self-confidence and satisfaction, thus also improving emotional control and concentration.

The Goal Setting Process

1. *Set the goal*
   - Develop goals systematically
   - Long- and short-term goals
   - Adjust goals for training and competition
   - Optimize goal difficulty
   - Is the focus of your goals appropriate?
2. *Develop goal commitment*
   - Taking responsibility
3. *Construct action plans*
   - Barriers to goals
4. *Obtain feedback*
   - Monitor and evaluate (goals and attainment)
5. *Reinforce goal achievement*

A rider's individual personality is likely to influence how different types of goal are set, and these types fall into three categories: outcome, performance and process orientated:

● Outcome goals are other-referenced, and involve winning (and losing) or beating an opponent, and depend in part on the ability of the opponent.
● Performance goals are self-referenced, and involve personal performance standards, under the rider's control – for example, less than a 60 per cent dressage test.
● Process goals are self-referenced and involve the performance of a particular skill, such as jumping a fence height; these are often used in training sessions, and are self-regulating.

All types may be relevant and may be appropriate to different specific goals, but the process is the same whichever is worked towards. Riders often like to see their performance assessed through a direct outcome, but the problem with setting this type of goal is that the outcome is not dependent upon our own performance. These outcomes relate to other competitors, so as a rider we can perform beyond our expectations and still not achieve a perceived outcome, consequently generating negative emotions on the performance.

Another aspect may be that we perform badly in a competition, but the other competitors were less skilled, which produces a successful result on the day but again does not truly reflect the training and how the training is progressing. Performance goals are much more robust measures during competitions, and process ones are very beneficial in the training environment where skill development is being undertaken.

Setting the types of goal will depend on the personality of the rider and what motivates

each individual. It is a huge commitment to own, look after and train a horse for relatively few competitive days. Individual commitments vary from someone wishing to pursue their dreams, be the best that they can be, develop and learn new skills, or enjoy the desire to continue to learn. These feelings in return allow us the feelings of enjoyment, the desire to feel competent and to develop pride in our progression.

Achieving the goals that have been set allows the rider to develop their confidence in their skills and ability to perform and achieve. This develops the belief in their own potential, their awareness of how they prepare, and their ability to achieve goals and overcome obstacles.

PSYCHOLOGICAL EXERCISES

The following exercises are suggestions that a rider can use if they feel it is appropriate to improve their awareness of how they deal with nerves or anxiety; it also gives them the opportunity to build up a written 'diary' of their performances in a retrospective reflective account (how you thought you did, and how it made you feel). They have been partly completed as examples, but working templates are available in the Appendix.

Exercise 1: Developing Self-Confidence

These are important skills to develop within our awareness of our riding skills. By addressing these three questions, self-talk can be learnt to improve confidence levels. It is not unusual to tell others how we feel but to tell ourselves more critical things, but being consciously aware of our thoughts can improve our awareness of our confidence levels and subsequently our ability to perform and handle the pressure of an event. The first step to developing self-confidence is to start to value yourself as a person and feel that you are important and need looking after. Riders are notoriously good at looking after and valuing their horses, but very poor at valuing themselves.

Key questions that a rider can address for themselves should be applied into a riding situation and practised on a regular basis and certainly before a competition. The following is a self-confidence work sheet, with some examples of responses.

Initially working through this simple work session may be an uncomfortable process. It is human nature, and particularly normal for riders, to tell themselves everything that they cannot do. It is therefore vital when developing self-confidence to change this awareness to what you *can* do, and to start to value yourself as an athlete. Initially this work sheet should be included at an early stage in the development of psychological skills, as it will take a little while before it feels a comfortable process, and can be used subsequently as a positive psych record of our performance. The other aspect about writing your feelings down is that they affirm your thoughts, which makes them more real and true to the person. By having a record of what you felt over a period of time will also help to counter any self-doubt that may creep in.

Date: **Event:**

List three reasons why you trust yourself as a rider

1.   *I trust my horse*
2.   *I have a secure lower leg (most of the time)*
3.   *I work and train hard*

List three reasons why you believe you are a good rider

1.   *I am naturally confident in my jumping ability*
2.   *My horse likes me*
3.   *I get good rider marks in my dressage test sheets*

List three reasons why it is important to look after yourself

1.   *I need to be able to work*
2.   *I don't want to let my horse down*
3.   *I want to be in the best place to do my best*

Exercise 2: Reflection Sheet, Analysis of Performance

REFLECTION SHEET (COMPLETED)

Event: Date:	Event results: Comments:
What went well about the day and why?	*I was organized and got to the event earlier than normal; this allowed me to feel better and more prepared particularly in the dressage and I got a better score of 31 penalties*
What would you like to to have changed and why?	*I could have given myself more time to get tacked up for the dressage as a little short of warm-up time*
If you could change anything, what would it be?	*To manage my preparation time better*

What have I learnt about:

1. Myself	*That I can be organized when I prepare early enough*
2. My horse	*That he is better behaved if I am calmer*
3. My worries	*I still get nervous about the dressage phase which makes me fuss more when I am getting ready*
4. Handling pressure	*I can cope with the pressure if I feel more prepared*
How can I use what I have learnt in the future?	*To build in more time to get ready and to understand that I need this time to feel better prepared*
Do I need to develop more skills to put this into place? If so, what are they?	*Try to be organized. I need to action plan the day before I get to the event – that way when I get nervous I can try to keep to time and be better prepared on the day*
How do I now proceed, and what is the time scale?	*I can straightaway plan for the next event*

As for the first exercise, this sheet should be completed after a competition and a record of it kept in order that the rider can reflect back on their feelings and their performance over the event season. These sheets should be kept and looked at when there are moments of self-doubt or perceived poor performance. In this way the rider can see how much they have improved over time, as well as recognize what they have done to get better. The completed sheets from the event season should be used to support reflection at the end of the season and help set realistic goals for the following year.

Exercise 3: Performance Profiling

Sheet 1: Dressage Performance Assessment

Although this is not a psychological skill it is useful for any rider to have an awareness of where they are within their skill set and what they need to do to develop improvements through training. There are quite a few profiling templates available and the one reproduced here is an example of how a skill set can be represented to develop performance skills. A rider can design their own but either way the principles are the same.

PERFORMANCE ASSESSMENT GRID (COMPLETED): DRESSAGE

Characteristic/skill Date:	Centre line	Halts	Trot left rein	Trot right rein	Canter left	Canter right	Trot circles	Canter circles	Transitions
10									
9									
8		■							
7		■		■	■	■		■	
6	■	■	■	■	■	■		■	
5	■	■	■	■	■	■	■	■	■
4	■	■	■	■	■	■	■	■	■
3	■	■	■	■	■	■	■	■	■
2	■	■	■	■	■	■	■	■	■
1	■	■	■	■	■	■		■	■

For the dressage phase a profiling sheet can be drawn up to assess the rider's current skills, and their ability to produce them in competition. The sheet should be completed from the rider's perspective, but it is useful to compare how the rider feels against some of the movements assessed within the tests themselves. In the sheet above the results suggest that the transitions are the weakest aspect of the test, that the horse is more consistent on the right rein, and that although the centre line may not be great, the halts are reliable. Profiling how the rider feels against the marks in the test can help them realize where they need to go in their training, as well as considering how the judge perceives the similar movements. As the season progresses a fresh grid can be produced and progress can be measured by comparing the development up the numerical scale. The profiling template can also be used for more general psychological skills that reflect individual progress (*see* Sheet 2).

Sheet 2: General Personal Performance Assessment

PERFORMANCE ASSESSMENT GRID (COMPLETED): CROSS-COUNTRY

Characteristic/skill — Date:	Confidence in self	Time management	Dressage skills	Jumping skills	Cross-country skills	Handling pressure	Competition nerves		
10									
9		■							
8		■			■				
7		■			■				
6		■	■		■				
5	■	■	■		■				
4	■	■	■	■	■	■			
3	■	■	■	■	■	■	■		
2	■	■	■	■	■	■	■		
1	■	■	■	■	■	■	■		

The list of characteristics/skills should be made personal and relevant to the needs of the individual rider. A rider's feelings are personal to them, and as such the columns should reflect the individual concerns. It is good practice to draw up a profile sheet before the competition season begins in order that the initial level of skills and confidence can be assessed. As the training sessions get under way and the skill sets improve, then the levels of achievement should change. Ideally the profiling sheet should be revisited after a reasonable time scale of four to six weeks has passed. As for all of the psychological assessments, records should be kept for later reflection: that way a person is able to see and recognize how much they have improved, and how their personal journey for self-development has occurred.

7 Competition Considerations

COMPETITION ENTRIES

You will no doubt be familiar with making entries for equestrian competitions. Part of your training and preparation will have involved competing in the individual disciplines, possibly at affiliated but more likely at unaffiliated competitions. Choosing the horse trials you wish to compete at and making an entry is important, and should not be left until the last minute.

British Eventing produces a bi-monthly schedule which gives the details of every BE and FEI event that takes place during that period. Their website also holds the schedules for every event planned to be held in the current year. You will need to choose the events you want to compete at, and make your decision according to how far away each event is, whether it is suitable for your level of ability, and the date the competition is to take place. There are also other excellent sources of information that will give you an insight as to what to expect at a particular event. *Eventing* magazine produces a comprehensive directory to each event which includes details of the cross-country course, the percentage of clear cross-country rounds, and useful comments from riders who have competed there. The Eventing Worldwide website also has an excellent photo gallery of the cross-country fences at each venue, which provides a guide to the complexity of a particular course.

Once you have made a shortlist of the events you may want to compete at, make a note of them in your diary; you should also include the date when the entries open and close, and the ballot date. You may also want to use the 'My Event Diary' section of the British Eventing website, which will help you manage your calendar and events.

When making an entry to an affiliated competition it is important to make sure that your entry arrives in good time and contains the correct information. All too often a competitor is disappointed when their entry is not accepted and they are unable to compete. The entry should not arrive before the opening date for entries, nor should it arrive after the closing date. If the event has a history of being oversubscribed and has to ballot, make sure your entry arrives before the ballot date: the ballot decides who cannot be accepted. Remember that the entries secretary for an event will have many entries to process, and the first to be discarded will be those that are incorrectly completed or are not sent with the correct payment. This is primarily due to the constraints on their time, as it takes more effort to contact a competitor and ask for the correct information than it does to process a correctly completed entry.

There are two ways to enter an affiliated competition: by post on the form issued by British Eventing, or online. Most events now offer online entries, and this is the way most secretaries prefer to receive them: it is instant, the details are automatically uploaded to the computer, and payment is received at the point of entry with no need for cheques to be processed. From the competitor's perspective, not only are the benefits the same, but also all the details for both rider and horse will be held on the website, so there will be no need for endless typing – nor will you have to rely on the postal service.

Make sure that you complete all the questions asked on the entry form: the name of the event, the date on which you wish to compete, and the class are regularly missed out when completing the hard copy entry form. Horse and rider details must be completed in full and legibly: many a competitor has been disappointed to find their name incorrectly spelt in the programme and on the scoreboard because their writing is illegible. If you have any special requests, state them clearly on the form. Be sure to complete the commentator information: this is used at the event, not only to announce details for each competitor but also to assist with the provisional scoring. You may think that you have nothing significant to say about yourself or your horse, but even the simplest piece of information is better than nothing at all, which will leave the commentator with no option but to say nothing. A good example would be 'First season competing with BE having successfully competed at the Riding Club Championships in 2011. Work as a fulltime nurse to fund my competing.' If you don't have a sponsor you could take the opportunity to thank those who support you – your parents or a long-suffering partner.

You need to include contact details, both a daytime and evening contact number, also details of your lorry or vehicle and trailer, and two emergency contacts should you have an accident. If you have qualified for the final of a series or a championship, details of your qualifying runs must be provided on the reverse of the form. You may also be eligible for a special prize, details of which appear in the schedule, for example 'The Johnny Morris trophy for the highest placed rider living in

the county of Herefordshire'. Most importantly don't forget to pay at the time of making your entry.

As mentioned above, some of the more popular events will be oversubscribed, in which case some competitors will be balloted out. Details of whether an event balloted in the previous year will be included in the schedule. You are more likely to be guaranteed a run if you choose an event which does not have a history of balloting, or if you compete at mid-week events. You will be issued with ballot stickers for your horse, which can be used to help you gain entry to an event. You will have one ballot sticker per horse per month, each printed with the month they are to be used in, from March through to October. You will also be allocated two 'Super Special Entries' which can be used at any time during the season. If you use one of these your entry cannot be balloted out, so they should be used for a particular event which you really want to go to. If you know that an event is likely to be popular and will therefore ballot, use your ballot sticker. Sometimes an event is so oversubscribed it even has to ballot out entries with a ballot sticker attached, in which case your entry form will be returned with the events stamp on it, and you can then use this returned form as a Super Special Entry with a future entry.

As the majority of events now use an online system you should be able to monitor the progress of your entry online: you will be able to find out the provisional timetable, your competitor number and section, and closer to the event, your competing times for each phase. If you need to telephone for times this will be stated in the schedule.

Once you have made your entry you probably won't need to have any further communication with the secretary; however, should you need to contact them, make sure you have all the correct information to hand. Again you need to remember that you are one of many competitors, and the entries secretary can't be expected to remember everyone's details when they call. Have your number, section and class to hand, and give your horse's name clearly. Be reasonable with your expectations: it is unfair to expect your times to be altered just because you forgot to mention that you needed late times. Many secretaries prefer to be contacted via email so they can reply in their own time.

If the event has to be abandoned due to adverse weather, details will be published on the British Eventing website and also on the telephone hotline. In some cases you may be contacted via a text message.

CHECKLIST FOR HORSE AND RIDER

Horse	*Rider*
Saddle – dressage/jumping	Jacket, gloves – dressage/jumping
Girths, numnahs and spares	Jodphurs + spare pair
Bridle – dressage/jumping	Boots, spurs
Breastplate/martingales	Shirt (+ spare), tie/stock and pins
Travel kit – rugs, boots, bandages, leather headcollar	Stick – schooling, jumping
for travelling + rope, tail bandage + guard	Cross-country colours/jumper
Studs – various types depending upon the ground	Body protector
conditions, stud tap and stud plugs	Hats, hairnet
Boots/bandages – SJ/XC/over-reach boots	Number bib
Clean and complete grooming kit	Medical card (complete) and armband
Plaiting kit	Stopwatch (Novice level and above)
Rugs – sweat/cooler/waterproof	Dry/clean clothes for travelling back in

Essential – should live in the lorry/trailer	*Extras – May live in the lorry/trailer*
Horse passport – vaccination details: it is illegal to travel	Boot cleaning kit
a horse without his own passport (DEFRA regulations)	Spare clean clothes
Tack cleaning kit	Money – start fees
Spare bridle	Mobile phone (charged)
Spare shoes	Map/SatNav
Spare headcollar and rope	Rule book
Spare rugs – waterproof, sweat, travel, warm	Dressage test
Full water container (fresh), buckets	Confirmation letter/directions/times
First aid kit (human and horse)	Wellies for walking the course when wet
Leg ice – coolant for after XC	Waterproofs – trousers and coats
Haynet, maybe hard feed	Food and drink – flasks or cold drinks, water
Wash bucket, sponge and scraper	Lunge line
Skip and tools	Neck strap
	Hole punch
	Electrician's tape (black/coloured
	if needed)

Remember to check before leaving home if you are in any doubt. If you make your entries within the published time frame, and communicate clearly and politely, you should not experience any problems and will be able to compete at your chosen events and will find the experience enjoyable and rewarding. Don't forget that all the officials and organizers are there to help you, so ask when you need assistance, and thank them afterwards.

THE DAY BEFORE

You will need to know what time you are competing, and times are normally made available either by telephone or through the internet a couple of days before the event. You should have a general idea of your start time from the information on your confirmation letter, but having the exact times for the three phases will enable you to plan your travel times, your warm-up time, and when you will have time to walk the course.

The Day Before Checklist

- Check vehicle – fuel, tyres, battery (in cold weather), oil and water, windscreen washer, lights, horse travelling area.
- Check the travel route, looking out for weather changes, roadworks. The journey may be longer by motorway, but it will give the horse a better ride than taking the shortest journey by 'A' roads.
- Pack the vehicle – all kit on the list that cannot be damaged by cold or risk being stolen can be packed the day before.
- Wash the horse, particularly the white bits; even if they need washing again in the morning, this will save time. It may be prudent not to wash the mane/tail because if it is very clean it can be slippery and hard

to plait; however, it should not be dirty and scurfy either, so you could plait it when it is just washed and still wet.
- Check stud holes: clean and tap them out, and repack with oiled cotton wool.
- Check, clean and prepare all competition tack and equipment.
- Plait the night before if the horse is stabled and not likely to rub them out; this is useful if you have an early start in the morning.
- Check your rider kit – maybe pack it all into a holdall and put it in the lorry if it is safe to do so.
- Check and pack spare equipment in the vehicle.

Working out Your Times – Backwards!

The table on page 142 is an example of how times can be worked out, and it is down to every individual to decide how much time they need. At some events there will be time to walk the course between phases; sometimes this will need to be built into the schedule before the dressage phase. Every event needs to be considered for its own timings, as well as factoring in variables such as the weather. Initially start with the cross-country start time, and then build backwards, depending upon your own needs.

Travel

The British weather and the roads are two things that can be relied on to be unreliable so it is important to plan ahead. Check the forecast the day before: if the event is some distance away the weather can be quite different from that at home. Be prepared by allowing extra travel time in poor weather. If the event is more than three hours away it may be more appropriate to travel the day before and stable overnight. This should be

WORKING OUT YOUR TIMES

Dressage = 10.00, Show-jumping = 12.58, Cross-country = 14.16

Activity	Time
Cross-country start time	14.16
Warm up cross-country	13.50
Tack up cross-country	13.30
Show-jumping start time	12.58
Warm up show-jumping	12.30
Tack up show-jumping	12.15
Walk XC course – allowing an hour	10.45
Dressage test start time	10.00
Warm up	09.20
Tack up allowing time for rider to get ready	09.00
Arrive at event and declare at secretaries, time to familiarize with event and walk show-jumping course	08.00
Travel time takes 1hr 15min – 1hr 30min, so allow 1hr 30min in case of delays, therefore need to leave yard at 6.30am	06.30
Load horse and build in extra time (30min) if running late	06.00
However long it takes you to get up, and get to the yard	?

considered at the time of entering the event, and then your decision made once you have confirmation of entry acceptance.

ON THE DAY

One of the simplest ways to check that all is going to plan and that you don't forget anything is to make a list of the things that you need to take for both you and your horse, as well as a 'To Do' list for the particular event. The checklist for horse and rider can be used for every event, as the equipment is unlikely to change. Most of us event for fun, and it is important that we have our friends around us to help and assist – but friends and family should never be taken for granted, and whether they are partners or friends, you should check that they are free to help at the

event. They, too, need to know your times for the day, and what time you need them to be ready to leave; they also need to know how long the day will be, as they probably have other commitments besides being your support team!

Once you arrive at the event, if possible you should consider how you park your vehicle: if it is hot try to find any natural shade, if windy or raining then you should consider which way your ramp opens so the rain doesn't come straight into the vehicle. A little adjustment when parking can also make the vehicle more level and comfortable for the horse, which may be standing inside it for some time. However, you may be told where to park by an official event steward, in which case you won't have any choice in the matter.

Once parked, drop the ramp and check that your horse has travelled safely; make sure he

EXAMPLE 'TO DO' LIST

- Put fuel in the lorry/ towing vehicle – ideally enough to get there and back.
- Take an appropriate map and directions, taking into account the weather (if adverse), roadworks, motorways and A roads, height or weight restrictions for lorries, and specific directions given by the event.
- Remember to take your purse/handbag/ wallet/money/phone (fully charged) – all last-minute essentials.
- Take the horse's passport, the event confirmation paperwork, and the BE rule book, which has the dressage tests in it.
- Pack the vehicle with all the horse's kit and your own.
- Take food and drink – for the horse and the rider, who is often forgotten.

is settled, then take time to familiarize yourself with the venue.

After settling your horse, you should then go to the secretary's tent as you will need to declare, show your horse's passport and your confirmation letter, pay your start fee and check your start times. In return you will be given your competitor's number and a programme. You can also find out when the show-jumping course is available for walking, as the organizers will have factored in course-walk times throughout the day. If this is your first event, take your jumping hat as it will need to be checked to make sure it is safe and of a suitable standard; a hat with a harness is also a requirement for the dressage phase in BE80, 90 and 100 classes. Once approved, it will be tagged. If you have an exo body cage protector you should inform the secretary so that the officials on the cross-country are aware of it in case of an accident. Should

you be travelling on your own then you will need to inform the secretaries of your vehicle registration and details in case there is an accident. Check the scoreboards and that you are in the right section, and that your and your horse's names are correctly spelt.

Whilst walking about, check where the collecting rings are for each of the phases: designated horse walkways may not be so obvious when you are riding from the lorry park to the collecting rings. Other considerations are to find the toilets, and to find out if the event has any distractions that may impact upon the performance of either the horse or the rider!

Walking the Cross-Country Course

If you have not already walked the cross-country course the day before, then you will need to do so on the day; this may be done before the dressage, although it will depend upon your times for each of the phases. You will need to allow at least an hour to walk the course, and ideally have an hour before the start of the dressage to have plenty of time to be prepared. When walking the course, take your programme

FEEDING AND FORAGE AT AN EVENT

Hay or haylage and water should be available or offered to your horse whilst at an event, although he should not be allowed forage for an hour before the cross-country otherwise it will be impacting on his digestive system when he is expected to compete with maximum effort. He can only have his hay back after he has returned from the cross-country and has totally recovered – has stopped blowing and has cooled down: this may take between fifteen and thirty minutes, depending upon the individual horse.

with you as this will list your course, the layout, the colour of your fence numbers, and how many fences there are. It is worth checking with the secretary that the course is as published, as fences may have been taken out due to safety issues, or altered if the weather has caused a last-minute change to any aspect of the ground or the course.

When walking the line to any of the fences, you should try to think how the horse will see the fence: this is very important through combinations or in fence complexes where there are various fences that are flagged for jumping in all the classes. The first impression can be confusing for the horse, and this should be considered when you approach the line of the fence. Remember that you will have the benefit of walking the course and knowing the lines that you want to take, but the horse will only see the fence and the line when you turn towards the fence. With this in mind, you need to walk the line of the course that you intend to ride; this is not the time to take shortcuts, or to assume that you know the lie of the course from where it ran last year. Whilst walking the course consider the ground conditions so that you can decide what sort of studs would be best to use (if any). Before leaving the cross-country course, take a moment and run through the whole course in your mind so that you visualize the fences, your line, and the speed of your approach to the jumps.

Depending upon what time of day it is when you walk the course, the ground and the weather may change. The sun and shadows may be in a different place if you are running later in the day, and so the fences may appear different on their approach. If after walking the course you are confused or worried about an aspect of the track or a fence, then you should return to the secretary's tent and ask them to explain the fence; either they or the steward or the technical adviser (TA) will be able to check

the detail with you. The rider representatives are another point of contact: these are riders who are competing at the event and are experienced competitors. They are available to support other riders and answer competitor queries about the course. Their names and general location (usually in the lorry park) will be stated at the secretary's tent.

The Dressage Phase

When returning to the lorry, try to be as normal as possible in getting your horse ready. He doesn't need his routine changing too much, so be quiet and calm around him. Tack up in the normal way that you would at home. Depending upon the weather you may need to get him ready in the vehicle, though take care that he doesn't squash you against the sides of the vehicle; it may be safer to put on his back boots, take off his tail bandage and oil his feet once you get him out of the vehicle. You will also need to put in his back studs when he is out of the vehicle.

Once he is tacked up you should consider your own turnout. When working in you need to be comfortable, but also ready to present yourself in the arena without too much fuss and preparation. If it is raining, then you could wear a waterproof coat over your jacket, or you will have to change into your jacket – your friend might help you change and put on your number bib before you go in. If hot, then wear a suitable breathable shirt that fits properly and can keep you cool. Before leaving the lorry park make sure that any equipment is secured in your vehicle, and that it is locked to avoid any casual opportunity for thieves.

On arrival at the collecting ring you should check in with the steward, find out which is your arena, and ask if the class is running to time and which horse you follow: this way you can plan your working in accordingly.

The aim of working in is to warm your horse up appropriately and ask him to come on to your aids: it is not a time to be schooling. It is useful to ride through a few movements that may be required in the test, but it is more important to have the horse working in good balance and being responsive to you as his rider, establishing his and your concentration on the work ahead. A good idea when in the collecting ring is to find a small area to warm up: all too often the rider drifts around the field working in large circles and with a lot of room, and the arena of 20 x 40m then feels very tight. Try to limit your working area to support the movements required in the test; this also supports concentration and minimizes the risk of bumping into other riders. When warming up, establish a plan at home, and try to keep to it when you are at a competition, as this will help you to stay focused and to perform well without overworking the horse.

You should know your and your horse's needs, so if he is relaxed about taking a break then finish working in and give him a rest; this gives you a chance to sort out your jacket and number and any other finishing touches. Take off your horse's boots and tail bandage, and remember that a schooling whip is not allowed in the arena. If your horse does not respond well to a break, then this should be factored into your warming up so that you arrive at the collecting ring suitably dressed and mentally prepared. Quietly think about the test and how you are intending to ride it. Gather your thoughts, and go in and give your horse the best ride you can to show the judge what you are able to do – basically at this point be positive and perform well.

The Show-Jumping Phase

After the dressage phase you should return to the lorry and prepare for the show jumping.

Times can be quite tight between phases, although there should be at least thirty minutes between each section. Quietly untack your horse and wash him down if needed, and make him comfortable, either putting him back on the lorry, or tying him to the outside of the vehicle (as long as he is not left unattended); this is sometimes the better option if he is wearing studs, as these can rip the rubber lining of the vehicle floor. He may need some sort of rug as protection against the flies/sun/rain. Check that his shoes are all secure – if they need attention there is normally a farrier on site, contactable through the secretary and usually located in the lorry park.

Make sure you leave yourself enough time to tack your horse up again, and to fit his boots and any other equipment. Once he is tacked up, then tie him back up again – as long as he is quiet to do so – and get yourself ready. You may need a different whip or gloves, or to make minor changes to your own attire. When you are ready, make your way down to the show-jumping collecting ring in plenty of time before your round.

When you get there inform the steward that you have arrived, check if the class is running to time, and find out who you follow (in the same way as for the dressage phase). You have already done your dressage test so the horse shouldn't need a long time warming up for this phase: remember this is not the time or place to train him, but simply to get him listening to your aids. Allow him time to settle, and work him in, paying particular attention to the quality of the canter. When he is sufficiently on the aids, then you can jump a few fences. The practice jumps are flagged with a red and a white flag to indicate in which direction the fence must be jumped: the red on the right and the white on the left; the different coloured tape on the wings corresponds to the different classes and denotes the maximum height for each class that may be jumped in the collecting ring.

It is best to start by jumping a cross-pole, then jump an upright a couple of times before raising the height. If all is going well you can move to the oxer, jumping it at a relatively low height before raising it to the height of the class. It is useful to finish your practice session by jumping the same shape of fence as the first fence on the course (usually an ascending oxer); this way you can mentally prepare for it with regard to the canter and the type of jump that you expect from the horse.

This whole process should only take as much time as it takes for a few horses to jump their rounds; many people spend too long jumping in the collecting ring. This is a useful place to have a helper: they can confirm with the steward how many horses are left to jump before you, so you can gauge the time that you actually need to warm up over the fences. Then your helper can assist in positioning themselves at the right fence for you and increase the heights when you are ready to do so. Planning how to ride in the collecting ring is a useful skill to learn at home as it reduces any miscommunication with your helper and keeps those nerves at bay. If you need to watch a few riders jump the course before you, then ideally this should be done before you start jumping in the collecting ring.

When you are called forward to enter the arena, you should already have decided which way you are going to approach the first fence. Keep an ear out for the judge's bell: when this has been rung you have forty-five seconds before you must go through the start, so there is time to establish a quality canter and make your way to the start gate without rushing.

When you go through the start, focus on the quality of the canter, your line and the next fence; try to enjoy your round because then you will ride well, with a positive attitude and focus. Should you have a problem and miss a fence, or have a technical elimination for an error of course, then you can ask the secretary if you are permitted to go on to the cross-country phase.

If you have been eliminated for refusals or a fall, this will not be permitted.

Once you have completed your round, return to the lorry and get ready for the cross-country.

The Cross-Country Phase

On returning to the lorry you should get yourself ready for the cross-country phase: you will need your cross-country colours, body protector, medical armband, whip and number bib. You then need to tack up the horse for the cross-country phase. If you use the same tack as for the show-jumping, then check that it still fits correctly and that your studs are still tight and suitable for the terrain. Put on the horse's cross-country boots, making sure that all the buckles or tapes are secured. Remember to shorten your stirrups to your cross-country length before you go down to the collecting ring.

When you arrive in the collecting ring, declare yourself to the steward – as in the other two phases – and find out if they are running to time. Times may vary: there might have been a hold on the course and things are running behind schedule, or the day may be running ahead of schedule due to riders withdrawing or not turning up on time. Occasionally a late change is made to the course: this can be checked with the collecting ring steward.

As for the show-jumping phase, you should warm up briefly: you have already completed two phases, so take care not to overwork your horse, particularly if it is a hot day. Once you have warmed up on the flat you need to jump the smaller of the practice jumps a couple of times from a straight line and from a more forward, ground-covering canter than you would have for show-jumping. When your horse is listening to you, move on to the next fence. After a couple of jumps it is sensible to approach either of the fences from a diagonal line, as you might on the course. Then take a brief rest and check your tack, as girths and nosebands can often become loose. Mentally run through the course in your mind – and then you are good to go!

As you are called forward to the start box, consider the needs of your horse, and whether he gets worried at the start. The starter will let you know when you have a minute left, then thirty seconds, and will count you down from ten seconds. At this point you can assess when you need to go into the box in order to make a controlled and confident exit from the box to start your cross-country phase. You should not be aiming to canter through the start box: if your horse is not going to walk in quietly and stand still, then speak to the starter and let them know that you intend to walk into the box at the last minute. The start team are there to help you, and are supportive if you let them know you need to do something different.

As you safely jump out of the start box it is important to keep focused on the first fence: all too often a horse is distracted and has a casual stop because the rider has presumed too much and not kept him focused and on the aids. As you successfully negotiate each fence you should straightaway be looking ahead to the next fence, keeping focused on the line and pace that you need. The quicker you can establish a rhythm after each fence, the earlier your horse will be able to go smoothly and quickly across country with no time penalties.

Occasionally you may get held on the course, perhaps because of an incident ahead of you on the track. The fence judge will flag you down with a red flag at a designated point and inform you that you are being held. These stopping points are situated around the course at the more straightforward fences, allowing you to confidently get going again when the course is clear. Whilst being held it is generally best to keep walking so that you and your horse are ready to get going again when the course is clear. If, however, there is a long delay you will be informed and you can dismount and rest; you should be given a couple of minutes warning when you will be started again. The fence judge will inform you of the exact point where your stopped time was taken, so when you can start again you should aim to establish your canter before that point so that in effect you pick up the course at the same pace. The fence judge will have noted your stopped time and your restart time, and the scorer will calculate your held time, and this will be deducted from your completed cross-country time, producing an accurate record of the time you have taken to get round the course.

It is important that you check the BE rules. At BE100 and below you are currently permitted to have four cumulative refusals on the course, whilst at BE Novice and above only three cumulative refusals are permitted on the course before the rider is eliminated. For any competition at any level a rider may only incur three refusals at any one fence before being eliminated. If this happens then it is your responsibility to leave the course at a walk and return to the lorry park.

On completion of the course you should pull up steadily and in balance. Dismount, loosen your girth and the noseband, and quietly lead your horse back to the lorry where he can be untacked properly and washed off; take care over his back if it is a very cold day as cold water can tighten the muscles. Once he has stopped blowing, his studs can be removed and his legs fully checked for any obvious knocks and cuts, and also rubs from his boots. Once washed off a suitable rug should be put on, such as a cooler in hot weather, and he should be led round to cool down properly; he can be offered a few mouthfuls of water every so often until his thirst is quenched, and he should be led around until he is fully relaxed and comfortable.

Once he has completely cooled down he can be offered a haynet. If you know he has a problem with his hydration status, or if he doesn't like drinking away from home, then the water offered can have electrolytes added (some horses will drink if a small amount of flavoured squash or cordial such as apple or mint is added). This is a very good way to encourage a fussy drinker as they taint the water with a taste that can be introduced at home so the horse becomes familiar with it and will then happily drink at an event. This is particularly important in hot weather when hydration can be a problem. If you need a vet then you should ask the secretary to contact him, informing them of where you are in the lorry park. You will be responsible for paying for any veterinary treatment that your horse may require.

Prize-giving

If you have any query with your score after you have finished then you should initially check the scores on the scoreboard and see if they correspond to your expectations. If you wish to raise a concern then you should first go to the secretary: if it is a mathematical query, they will check with the scorers and get back to you; if you wish to place a formal objection, this can be raised through the procedures laid out in the rule book.

If you have to stay at the event, perhaps to attend the prize-giving, then keep offering the horse water throughout the rest of the day. Once all the riders in your dressage section have completed their tests your sheets will be released from the secretary. Check your scores on the scoreboard to see how you have progressed, as well as where you usually finish within a section. If you are in the top ten then you will need to present yourself for the prize-giving in your show-jumping attire. Lastly, before leaving the event it is always polite and good practice to thank the secretary for all their hard work, and to show your appreciation for the event.

Travelling Home

In the excitement of the day it is easy to forget about the journey home. You may find yourself in a variety of emotional states, ranging from ecstatic as a result of having had a very successful day, and disappointed, tired and potentially injured or sore if you have had a fall. Whatever your state, it is important that you check on your health. Make sure you have eaten something and, more importantly, are well hydrated. All too often we look after the horse's needs but forget about our own.

Once the horse is comfortable after the event we should address our needs and the journey home. Eat and drink something, and repack the lorry. If there has been a gap between the end of the cross-country and the journey, and the horse has been standing on the lorry, then take him off and allow him to have a drink and a walk around and the opportunity to stale. Tack him up for travelling: a suitable rug for the weather and the journey, boots or bandages and tail bandage/guard. It is a matter of personal preference whether you travel your horse with a haynet, but it is much better for the horse if he can eat regularly, providing there is no reason that limits this on the way home, such as being a poor traveller.

At Home

When you get home and unload your horse, observe how he walks out of the vehicle. He should be calm and relaxed, sound and happy to be back. If all is well then he can return to his stable, have his travelling kit taken off and be rugged up with his stable rugs. Check his legs and general wellbeing. Depending upon the time of day you should unpack the vehicle or at the very least take out any valuable equipment such as the tack and your personal kit. Muck out the horse travelling area and return the vehicle to its usual place.

THE NEXT DAY

The day after a competition should be an easy day for your horse. At morning stables check his general wellbeing, his legs for any knocks, bumps or swellings that may have come up overnight. He should then have an easy day, either turned out in the field, or hacked out quietly if this is not possible. He should not be just left in his stable, as this will only encourage stiffness after the event.

Unpack the vehicle and clean it thoroughly if this was not done the day before. Check that the floor is clean and dry, particularly important if loose rubber matting is used. Then thoroughly clean all the event tack and equipment, replacing any that is worn or broken and repacking it in an organized manner. Repack the lorry with any competition equipment that can be stored in the vehicle so that it is ready for your next event.

8 The Next Level

With a sound, fit and able horse it is quite possible to progress through the various levels in eventing, and certainly to consider stepping up to the next level: this may be tackling your first Intermediate course, or competing in your first three-day event. However, it is important to be realistic about the expectations that you have for you and your horse, and also the skill level that you both possess. Some horses – and indeed riders – are quite content to stay at Novice level; furthermore some are very consistent up to a certain level but do not have the conformation to compete at a higher level, where the physical demands and expectations on the horse's athletic ability are much greater.

POTENTIAL LIMITATIONS

If a horse begins to struggle with the distances, speeds or technical demands at the next level, then problems will develop. Simple problems may be that the horse is no longer competitive due to the greater speed required for the cross-country phase. This sort of issue is likely with more heavily built horses, or those with a more common breed profile: whilst safe and sensible performers, they do not possess the athletic canter or galloping ability of the more Thoroughbred horse. They therefore jump relatively slowly round the track, accumulating time faults – or they might begin to show physical signs of wear and tear such as windgalls and minor lamenesses, or more serious soft tissue injury to tendons and ligaments.

Other horses may start to struggle with the technical aspects of the show-jumping, and begin having a pole down regularly. Whilst potentially irritating for the rider, when this happens it does not usually develop into a safety concern. Other horses start to lose confidence and may refuse at fences, or lose their trust in the rider. In this situation the health and safety of both the horse and rider is compromised, and the rider may have to concede that their horse has reached the limit of his ability. The rider must at all times be realistic about their own expectations set against the natural skill set and training level of their horse: after all, it is not the horse that has made the decision to compete or step up to the next level.

A basic error that riders often make is that they do not appreciate the technical demands of competing at the next level. The horse needs to be fitter, and so the rider will need to invest more time in his preparation and training, and to undertake this commitment in a more professional manner. Most horses have a reasonable skill set that enables them to jump up to 1.10m, but beyond this some natural ability, talent and support from technical training and fitness work is required.

Rider Limitations

Whilst the rider may be keen to progress,

good intentions alone are not always sufficient, and they do also need both the talent and aptitude for competing at a higher level because the technical demands of all three phases are that much greater. Thus the rider will need to show greater independence in their position for the dressage phase, and be quicker to think and react to the movements. Whilst in the show-jumping the fences are only 5cm (2in) higher, the oxers will be wider, and the lines and turns tighter and more technical. Finally the cross-country phase is more demanding: besides the increase in the fence dimensions, the course is longer (2,400–3,620m) with between twenty-two and thirty-two jumping efforts, and more complex in design, including where

the fences are sited and the influence of the terrain; lastly at 550mpm the speed is faster. All of these demands mean that the rider must be able to react more quickly, must be fit enough to be adaptable in their position, and have the mental resolve to want to put themselves through the additional demands of the higher level.

At Intermediate and one-star level the dressage test is equivalent to British Dressage Elementary level, so this is the level of training and way of going that the horse should be working at. The paces need to be correct (as for any level), but greater balance and expression should be seen as the horse becomes more supple and acceptance of the contact becomes more established. The horse should be secure

Fig. 8.1   Schooling for the next level.

to the rein, working with his head and nose just in front of the vertical, as in Fig. 8.1. The back should be soft and free from tension, allowing the connection from the energy created through the hind leg to come through to the contact, with a willing acceptance of the aids. The rider should be able to sit in balance in rising and sitting trot; although in this picture the rider is in balance, she has allowed her shoulders to come forward, when in fact she needs to engage more through her core to lift her upper body and sit taller.

THE FIRST INTERMEDIATE

It is quite natural for any rider to wish to progress to the next level of competition. The majority of non-professional competitors who event compete at Novice level and below, and it is the professional and semi-professional riders who fill the Intermediate classes and above to educate their horses with a long-term aspiration to four-star and team opportunities.

There are fewer opportunities for competing at Intermediate and above, and this needs to be factored in at the event planning stage: for example, the distance to travel, and where the event sits in the calendar in relation to other events should be considered. It is advisable to ask the horse to move up to the next level at a relatively straightforward 'first time' event, before he has 'officially' upgraded to Intermediate level; by this planning strategy if there is a problem at Intermediate level he has the option to compete back at Novice level, which is well within both horse and rider's comfort zone and partnership confidence can hopefully be re-established fairly quickly. If both horse and rider are comfortable at the new level then the Novice class can be used to become more competitive, with the quicker and more direct routes

being considered whilst trying to be as conservative as possible with the lines and the speed.

The Dressage

The Intermediate dressage test equates to a British Dressage Elementary level test, the horse now being expected to carry himself in a better balance throughout the test. The movements are expected to be executed at the markers rather than between them, and transitions within each pace are required, so the horse must be able to move confidently between the collected, working and medium paces, with some extension seen in the walk. The movements become more demanding, with 10m circles in trot and 15m circles in canter, and also reinback, and must be executed more accurately. Because the horse needs to be fitter than for Novice – largely due to the increased demands of the cross-country phase – he may have higher energy levels, and the downside of this is that he may find it hard to maintain concentration and relaxation in the dressage phase.

The difference in the show-jumping from BE Novice to Intermediate is the same as BSJA Newcomers to Foxhunter: the fences are higher and wider, and the course more technical including a treble, probably a dog leg, and more demanding related distances, and the materials used might include a water tray. The intention of this phase is to assess the athleticism and jumping ability of the horse, and the control and communication between horse and rider. As at Novice level, if too many penalties are incurred in the show-jumping, then horse and rider are not permitted to continue in the competition and go across country because they are considered to be a risk to their own health and safety.

The cross-country is run over a longer course, at a faster speed (550mpm) and with a greater number of jumping efforts, so the horse needs to be fitter, more responsive to the rider, and sufficiently confident to cope with the increased technical demands of the track. The horse's cardiovascular fitness will need to be increased to achieve the longer distances of Intermediate tracks, as will his aerobic fitness to cope with the faster speed requirements. Quite a few horses can cope with the fitness demands at Novice level without over-exertion, but at Intermediate level a specific training programme will be needed to address the cantering and galloping requirements.

For horses competing at Intermediate level and above, gallop exercise is therefore essential (some less athletic horses may require this at Novice level too, to enhance their general fitness), and the facilities at your home yard and the grassland type will determine whether the horse can do the necessary fastwork at home. If this is not possible he will need to go to a purpose-made gallops once or twice a week.

All these considerations must be factored into a training plan which will need to address the issues of time as well as additional expense, particularly if this involves transport to and from, and the hire of a gallops.

Canter Work and Fitness Preparation

For the horse to be fit, skilled and confident enough to compete at Intermediate level a consistent training programme should be worked out and followed. He should do some fast canter/galloping work at least twice a week, and this needs to have some structure to it so that the training plan is tailored to the individual horse's needs. Thus if he is naturally 'hot' or sharp then the canter work can be developed to incorporate steady canter periods to encourage him to settle and work at speed in a rhythm. If he is a little stuffy or thick in the wind, then the canter work can be carried out at a faster speed but over a shorter distance to encourage him to work more comfortably at the quicker Intermediate speed.

Whatever the type of fastwork undertaken, it is important that the ground conditions are good in order to keep the horse fit and sound. As discussed above, if you are fortunate enough to have access to good grassland then it may be possible to canter at home, but in order to be consistent with your training it may be necessary to work on a gallops.

When riding fastwork the rider should take the opportunity to improve their own fitness and co-ordination by riding at a shorter stirrup length. A good guideline is to ride a couple of holes shorter than you would for the cross-country phase. This will condition you to improving the strength and postural stability of your legs, as well as the cardiovascular demands of riding short and not taking any weight in the seat/saddle.

FASTWORK SCHEDULE

Day	Activity
Monday	Day off/rest day
Tuesday	Schooling on flat/hacking
Wednesday	Fastwork
Thursday	Hacking/easy schooling flat session
Friday	Jump schooling
Saturday	Hacking/light schooling
Sunday	Fastwork

Horses do not need to be training every day, but they do benefit from regular ridden work, particularly if they are stabled. If a horse is doing between 1–1½ hours of ridden work per day for five to six days per week he should be fit enough to compete at Novice level. Over the period of a week the routine will be made up of two fastwork sessions and two schooling sessions, one flat and one jumping. This programme can be tailored to the individual owner and horse, so in some situations an additional schooling session may be introduced or more hacking added if the horse's basic fitness needs to be improved. Ideally when designing a training programme the rider should work backwards from the intended event.

It is useful to have a fastwork day at the weekend, as this can be replaced with a competition day when working out a training plan over a few months. Every competition day will advance the horse's fitness and so should be factored into the training regime. If the horse is going to do some cross-country schooling to develop his education to the next level, then this day can replace a fastwork session – providing that you do undertake some fastwork, and don't just canter around jumping one fence at a time.

Training days can be changed a little, but it is important to give the horse an easier day after fastwork in order that any muscle or physical fatigue can be allowed to recover without excessive stress on the horse's body.

Horses (or schoolmasters) that in the course of their career have previously reached and maintained a higher fitness level will always find it easier to return to this condition, whereas a five- or six-year-old that is developing his training and fitness will initially take longer to reach the same fitness level.

THE FIRST THREE-DAY EVENT

The Fédération Équestre Internationale (FEI) is the organizing body for three-day events in the UK and worldwide. The first level is the CCI*, which is an international event equating to Novice level. There are various prerequisite qualifications that must be acquired as a measurement of a minimum achievement before entry is accepted into the competition. Primarily a horse and rider partnership should be jumping clear round a Novice cross-country course with only a few time faults; their show-jumping performance should be solid enough to jump round the 1.10m course with only a few penalties, and their dressage test must be completed with a minimum of penalties. However, it is good practice to be both training and competing at a higher level. The specific requirements are clearly stated in the British Eventing rule book, which is updated annually to include any recent changes. These standards are set in order that a horse and rider partnership achieves a basic level of safety and competence before their entry can be considered.

There are some unaffiliated three-day competitions that are organized according to British Eventing guidelines. The British Riding Club championships run over a three-day format at levels equating to BE100 and Novice standards. These competitions are an excellent way to start at a three-day level, and can also be used in a training programme for your first FEI one-star competition. To compete in the British Riding Club competition it is first necessary to become a member within your local Riding Club area. Regional qualifiers are held as regular one-day events and the team or individual riders must qualify to go through to the final championships in August. Qualifiers run on a regional area basis are often over BE courses; classes vary from Novice and Intermediate to Open level.

When stepping up to your first three-day event it is important to consider how it may be incorporated into the competition diary, and where it sits within your goal-setting strategies and time frame. As your first three-day competition it is often sensible to plan it towards the end of the competition season; this way there is plenty of time to adjust the training plan throughout the year with different objectives being set when competing, such as jumping some confident, clear cross-country rounds.

The training programme for your first

three-day event should factor in the same planning needs as for your first Intermediate. Although a horse and rider partnership does not need to have completed an Intermediate event as part of a one-star qualification, it should be considered within the training programme as it will expose the horse and rider combination to more technical demands and questions which they should be capable and confident of dealing with prior to their first three-day event. A training plan should be considered when the aims for the year have been completed (as part of the rider's goal-setting process).

The table below outlines a generic training plan for a one-star three-day event. This example is for a horse that is competing at Novice level and so is currently in work and fit enough to compete safely and confidently. The rider can adjust the schooling sessions to fit the individual horse's needs and their own work schedule. The canter sessions refer to the duration of canter followed by the rest period: therefore $6 \times 3 \times 5 \times 3 \times 6$

OUTLINE ONE-STAR EVENT TRAINING PLAN

Week	Monday	Tuesday	Wednesday	Thursday	Friday	Saturday	Sunday
1	Rest	School 30 min hack 60min	Fastwork $5 \times 3 \times 5 \times 3 \times 5$	Hacking/ easy session	Hacking easy school	Jump schooling	Competition $5 \times 3 \times 5 \times 3 \times 5$
2	Rest	School 30 min hack 60 min	Fastwork $5 \times 3 \times 5 \times 3 \times 5$	Hack 1½ hr	School 45 min hack 60 min	School 45 min hack 60 min	Fastwork $5 \times 3 \times 5 \times 3 \times 5$
3	Rest	School 30 min hack 60 min	XC school	Hack 1½ hr	School 45 min hack 60 min	Show-jumping competition	Fastwork $5 \times 3 \times 5 \times 3 \times 5$
4	Rest	School 30 min hack 60 min	Fastwork $5 \times 3 \times 5 \times 3 \times 5$	Hack 1½ hr	School 45 min hack 60 min	School 45 min hack 60 min	Fastwork $6 \times 3 \times 5 \times 3 \times 6$
5	Rest	School 30 min hack 1¼ hr	Fastwork $6 \times 3 \times 6 \times 3 \times 6$	Hack 1½ hr	School 45 min hack 60 min	School 45 min hack 60 min	Competition
6	Rest	School 30 min hack 1¼ hr	Fastwork $7 \times 3 \times 6 \times 3 \times 7$	Hack 1½ hr	Show-jumping competition	School 45 min hack 60 min	Fastwork $7 \times 3 \times 7 \times 3 \times 7$
7	Rest	School 30 min hack 1½ hr	Fastwork $7 \times 3 \times 7 \times 3 \times 7$	Hack 1½ hr	School 45 min hack 60 min	School 45 min hack 60 min	Fastwork strong gallop
8	School 30 min Hack 90 min	Fastwork, travel to event	Trot up, hack or gentle school	Dressage/ school or hack	Dressage/ hack	Cross-country	Vet's inspection SJ

equates to six minutes of cantering, followed by three minutes rest at walk, five minutes canter followed by a second three-minute rest at walk, and then a third session of six minutes (interval training). The cantering should be done at about 550mpm, depending on the horse and the ground; thus if a horse is working on the flat he may need to go faster than one doing hill work. The type of terrain that the horse is galloped on can vary according to its physical needs and temperament: thus if a horse tends to be lazy in his fastwork then it may help to gallop him alongside another horse to maintain and develop his enthusiasm and fitness.

The schooling and hacking sessions also need to be tailored to the horse's fitness and education. The hacking should be across a variety of terrain and include hillwork; this will build up stamina as well as reducing stress and strain on the forelimbs. The schooling sessions also need adjusting to accommodate the education and training needs of both horse and rider.

YOUR NEXT HORSE

If you are frustrated by the limitations of the horse you have, then it may be time for you to consider a more athletic type that will achieve the next level. However, bear in mind that horses with talent and athletic ability often require more attention and consistent management to support their physical and psychological needs. Not every competition horse will thrive in a DIY environment: they require consistency of routine, understanding of their temperament, regular work and a supportive stable management regime. However, if a more experienced or capable horse is the next step, then the following should be considered: his level of experience, his type, his jumping ability and his competition experience.

Level of Experience

It is important to consider your own personal needs and time commitments when proposing to compete at Intermediate level or higher. Whilst it is rewarding to be able to produce your own horse through the grades, working with a talented young horse requires a considerable amount of time and expertise, something that a professional rider can provide but which can be very hard for a single horse owner to achieve. A schoolmaster is another potential option: this can be a horse that has reached a good standard but may not go all the way to Advanced, but can still compete comfortably at Intermediate or one- and two-star level.

When looking at the schoolmaster option the horse's competition record should be carefully scrutinized: this will provide information about his performance in each of the phases, as well as his competition success and current form. Any periods of time off from competing should be investigated: there may be a genuine explanation, or it may be indicative of soundness issues that have curtailed the horse's progress, and which might make you wary of buying him.

The Type of Horse

If you are looking for a horse that will do more than your previous one, then by definition you should be looking for something that is different from your own horse. 'Different' should mean 'better' in terms of athletic ability – although in some respects the new horse will be similar: thus his height and build are likely to remain much the same, since you as a person have not suddenly got taller, smaller, heavier or lighter, so the new horse's size and shape may be similar to your previous horse. His temperament may also be similar, unless that of your original horse was particularly unsuitable, and he was either too laid back or too exuberant. However, a competition horse by its very nature is likely to be more alert and have high energy levels due to his fitness and training.

The breed may also be an influential factor, because as the eventing demands increase, so the athletic ability of the horse also needs to increase. Generally speaking the higher the level, the more Thoroughbred blood is desirable in the sport horse; however, one consequence of increasing the 'blood' may be that the horse's temperament is more excitable, which in turn may make him more difficult to train, which will be reflected in his performance.

Whatever the horse's type and temperament and whatever his competition record, soundness is a critical factor when purchasing a higher level competition horse. As the technical

Fig. 8.2   Standing up in hand: correct and suitable conformation for competing to the highest level.

Fig. 8.3   In movement: the potential Advanced young horse.

demands of the sport increase, so do the physical demands imposed upon the horse, and it is crucial that conformational traits that are perhaps lacking in the average horse are present in the performance horse in order that he remains sound, trainable and competitive. Figs 8.2 and 8.3 show a horse of correct, sound conformation that should enable him to compete to the highest level.

This bay gelding is the five-year-old, 16.2hh, ISH (Irish Sports Horse) and BYEH (Burghley Young Event Horse) finalist for 2010. BYEH is a national competition for four- and five-year-old potential event horses. The final is held at Burghley horse trials and many finalists have gone on to prove themselves as successful eventers. The demands of competing beyond Novice require a horse to be physically strong, sound and robust, and this horse is very pleasing to the eye: on first impression he looks symmetrical and balanced, with good body proportions and a well defined head, neck and shoulder. His shoulder angle matches his hoof/pastern angle, and he is well sprung through the ribs and strong across his back, suggesting that he will be able to develop suppleness and strength when he is in training. His limbs are also well proportioned, and his legs clean. His knees are flat and support a strong, short cannon bone. In the hind leg the hocks are strong and the lower limb is placed well underneath him. All of these factors indicate a correct and sound conformation that will enable this horse to compete to the highest level.

Fig. 8.3 demonstrates that he is just the stamp of horse that is desirable for Novice level and above. It is important to be able to assess the horse's conformation when he is standing up in hand, and relate it to him in movement. Thus in Fig. 8.2 we can see this horse standing up and looking strong and athletic, and when we see him ridden under saddle the same qualities come through. Here he is moving freely forwards in trot: as a

five-year-old he is still in the early stages of his education and development, but already he is showing athletic, free, forward movement, with a relaxed expression and way of going. When ridden the temperament of the horse often comes through more than when he is handled from the ground. This horse is very confident in his way of going, but still responsive to the rider's aids. When moving up to a higher level the horse should have a certain amount of character, but must still be compliant to the wishes of his rider.

Assessment of Jumping Ability

The event horse needs to be naturally scopey and must enjoy jumping: even at a young age the inherent skill and desire to jump should be apparent. However, it is important not to overface this type of horse in its early years, just because it can jump a big fence: it is far more important to focus on training, and developing the horse's canter. Having said that, if the horse is showing a natural talent and desire to jump it does not achieve a great deal to be jumping small fences, so a happy medium needs to be found.

As mentioned above, bringing on a young horse is time-consuming so a better option may be to invest in a schoolmaster – but whatever you decide, it is important to assess the horse's way of jumping. Figs 8.4–8.6 show a horse with a good jumping technique.

It can be quite hard to assess the whole picture of the horse when standing by the jump, so it is a good idea to focus on one aspect at a time. Fig. 8.4 shows the horse at the point of take-off, and we can see that he has placed his hind legs underneath his body and is pushing through his hocks in order to spring off the ground. His forearms have come forward and off the ground, but have not yet come up as a pair: this will happen as soon as his hind legs actually leave the ground and he is in

Fig. 8.4   Good style in take-off.

flight. The rider is in good balance, her contact allowing the horse the freedom of his head and neck, and her balance remaining behind the wither. Her lower leg is in an excellent position, with the weight firmly in the stirrup.

Fig.8.5 shows the horse in flight over the fence, with both knees brought up together as a pair. He is clearing the fence comfortably and is soft through his back, as is evidenced by the lowering of his neck and head, the lifting of his abdomen and the relaxed tail position. The rider is in good balance, allowing the horse the freedom to express his natural jump.

The last phase of the bascule is the landing: in Fig. 8.6 the left fore has just made contact with the ground, and the horse is bringing his

Fig. 8.5   A good bascule.

Fig. 8.6 Good style in landing.

head and neck up to stabilize the rotation of the back from the flight of the jump (note the height of the quarters at this point). The hind legs are being thrown up and backwards, indicating that he has made the correct technical shape over the fence (some horses will cramp their hind legs under their body, and this is a poor technique that is hard to improve). The rider is sitting up and off the horse's shoulders; in the next instant she will be bringing her lower leg forwards to take the weight and impact of the landing through her feet and legs. Her rein contact is allowing the horse the freedom to make a good jump, but she has not lost any control and is independent in her position.

Competition Experience

Many good competition horses are produced by professionals as a part of their business plan to sustain their eventing career. Professional riders need to ride and produce horses commercially for profit for owners, and to support their own eventing lifestyle. Eventing dealers will also provide a similar business, producing horses across all levels and then selling them on a commercial basis. Private owners, on the other hand, may have more personal reasons for selling a horse.

Whatever the type of yard you purchase your horse from, it is important to consider the build and ability of the rider who has produced and competed the horse. Thus if you are a lady of small frame and petite build and an amateur rider, it is probably not that wise to buy a horse from a heavily built, professional male rider who will inevitably ride the horse in a very different manner. Another consideration is that if the professional rider is very skilled at riding a variety of horses and training them correctly to a high level, then the horses they produce may well need riding to a similar standard in order to produce the same results. If you go down this road you need to be realistic about your own performance and abilities and take advice and maybe additional training to get to know your new performance horse and how to ride it.

The other option is to buy from an amateur rider, which may mean that although the horse has been produced less professionally, it may be more accommodating to a few rider mistakes.

Whatever the background and experience of your new horse, it will take some time for you to adjust to each other and develop a partnership. Just because a horse has a good competition record does not mean that it is either possible or a good idea to go straight into that level of competition. Various qualification regulations are set down by British Eventing and the FEI to ensure that a good relationship and safe partnership has been established at the lower levels before upgrading. If a schoolmaster has acquired too many points for the rider to compete him at a lower level – for example an Advanced horse in an Intermediate class – then it is possible to compete in either Open classes (for example Open Intermediate) or HC (non-competitively) until a safe and confident partnership has been established in the competition environment. It is also possible to downgrade a horse if it has not won any points in the current and preceding two calendar years. If this situation applies then the rider should contact British Eventing to request an application for downgrading. If a horse is downgraded, he will lose any previously acquired points and will be registered as a Grade 4 horse.

FINANCIAL CONSIDERATIONS

When stepping up to the next level many things must be taken more seriously, and this will have a cost factor, both in time and financially. Primarily this involves the costs of training – lessons, the hire of facilities such as a cross-country course for schooling, show-jumps and gallops – and the cost of travelling to events, whether for schooling purposes or to compete. A more rigorous fitness and training programme will need to be drawn up, bearing in mind that it is more beneficial to be training above the level that you are competing at, so it is worth investing in additional training support for you and your horse in order to make the event successful.

It is better to spend more time and effort in training so that you are prepared to your best advantage and therefore able to perform well. It achieves nothing to enter a class simply to 'have a go': not only is it not safe, but it is demoralizing and expensive to perform badly and risk elimination.

Further Information

Fédération Équestre Internationale (FEI)
www.fei.org
The FEI is the international governing body for all equine sports. It is an umbrella organization that works in conjunction with the national federation for each member country: for example the British Equestrian Federation. It is responsible for the running and governance of eventing on the world stage. The premier eventing competitions are the Olympic Games, the World Equestrian Games, FEI Classics, FEI World Cup Eventing and the Continental Championship. The three-day events that are run in the UK are organized according to FEI rules, and are classified according to a star rating, from one star (equivalent to international Novice level), two star (international Intermediate), three star (international Advanced) and four star (international World Championship level, such as Badminton, Burghley, Lexington and Kentucky). In addition there are classes categorized as CCI, which is an international three-day event, and CIC, which is an international one-day event; these classes are also star-rated from one to four stars.

British Equestrian Federation (BEF)
British Equestrian Federation
Stoneleigh Park
Kenilworth
Warwickshire
CV8 2RH
www.bef.co.uk

The BEF's mission statement is 'More people, more horses, more places, more medals'. The BEF is the national governing body for horse sports in the United Kingdom and speaks for all equestrian sports; it is the umbrella organization under which British Eventing sits, along with fifteen other organizations. The disciplines are eventing, show-jumping, dressage (including paralympics dressage), driving, endurance and vaulting, and the supporting organizations are the British Horse Society incorporating the Pony Club, approved British riding schools, the British Equestrian Trade Association, the British Reining Horse Association and the Scottish Equestrian Association.

British Eventing (BE)
National Agriculture Centre
Stoneleigh Park
Kenilworth
Warwickshire
CV8 2RN
www.britisheventing.com

This is the national governing body within the United Kingdom and has responsibility for the running and governance of the national one-day competitions, qualifying competitions for the FEI events, and the training and education of horses and riders from grass roots to world class level. A rule book is produced annually which gives updates on any FEI changes, as well as clearly stating the rules and regulations of all the national classes. For riders looking for training support, British Eventing provides a comprehensive training programme and coaching structure with accredited trainers who are qualified and insured, and maintain their professional development through organized training days.

British Riding Clubs (BRC)
British Riding Clubs
Abbey Park
Stareton
Kenilworth
Warwickshire
CV8 2XZ
www.britishridingclubs.co.uk

There are over 430 affiliated riding clubs and riding centres around the UK. The objectives of the BRC movement are:

- To assist and encourage those interested in the horse.
- To improve and maintain the standard of horsemanship.
- To improve the welfare of the horse.

This organization is structured around regional riding clubs that offer training and local competitions, which then provide qualification to the BRC National Championships. The majority of their classes and regional competitions are often organized over BE courses and so offer excellent training and competitive experience within local areas. The levels of competition often equate to BE classes (*see* table on page 166).

The BRC hunter trials start with classes at a maximum height of 75cm or 85cm. Classes range from Novice, pairs and Intermediate; there are also sections involving teams and individuals. The BRC national horse trials have the following classes: Senior Novice, Senior Intermediate, Senior Open, Junior Novice and Junior Intermediate. At the National Championships the Senior Intermediate and

Senior Open classes take place over three days, with the addition of roads and tracks and the steeplechase phases to the cross-country day. The Senior Novice takes place over two days, with roads and tracks and the steeplechase included. The Open section is equivalent to BE Novice at approximately 1.10m.

The Pony Club (PC)
The Pony Club
National Agriculture Centre
Stoneleigh Park
Kenilworth
Warwickshire
CV8 2RW
www.pcuk.org

The Pony Club is an international voluntary youth organization for youngsters interested in riding. Many of the most successful event riders started at a grass roots level with the PC. The objectives are:

- To encourage young people to ride and learn to enjoy all kinds of sports connected with horses and riding.
- To give instruction in riding and horsemanship and to educate members to look after and to take proper care of their animal.
- To promote the highest ideals of sportsmanship, citizenship and loyalty to create strength of character and self discipline.

There is an Open Eventing League which aims to encourage members to compete at Open level, and provides an opportunity to practise at this level as a preparation for the Area competitions and championships. Running under Pony Club eventing rules (Level 5), the show-jumping and cross-country are at 1.10m, which is the equivalent of BE Novice. The classes are open to all horse and rider combinations except BE Grade 1 horses (holding sixty-one points or more). They must be suitably qualified to compete. Most of these competitions are run over BE courses.

EQUIVALENT PONY CLUB TO BRITISH EVENTING CLASSES

Level	Pony Club	British Eventing
Level 3:	Novice	BE90
Level 4:	Intermediate	BE100
Level 5:	Open	BE Novice

The British Association of Equine Dental Technicians (BAEDT)
www.baedt.com

The British Association of Equine Dental Technicians (BAEDT) was founded in 2001 and is an organization for qualified professional equine dental technicians, promoting the professional training of technicians and providing greater understanding of the need for equine dentistry to the general public. Veterinarians and practising EDTs realized that there was a great need for a recognized examination and code of conduct for those who wished to look after horses' teeth. This was to give the horse-owning public and vets a list of people who have been rigorously examined by the British Equine Veterinary Association (BEVA) and the British Veterinary Dental Association, and have agreed to abide by performing guidelines and a code of conduct, and who are fully insured.

This Association represents many of the freelance equine technicians that are readily available for owners to use to get their horses' teeth checked. Both vets and dentists are qualified to assess and support the dental needs of your horse. A horse should have annual checks to his teeth, and if there are any usual developments then more regular checks may be recommended. These checks will support the conformation of the horse's mouth from both a nutritional aspect (being able to eat properly) and a training perspective (accepting the bit and nosebands comfortably).

Appendix
Useful documents

SELF-CONFIDENCE WORK SHEET

Date: **Event:**

List three reasons why you trust yourself as a rider:

1.

2.

3.

List three reasons why you believe you are a good rider:

1.

2.

3.

List three reasons why it is important to look after yourself:

1.

2.

3.

REFLECTION SHEET, ANALYSIS OF PERFORMANCE

Event: **Event results:**

Date: **Comments:**

What went well about the day and why?

What would you like to have
changed and why?

If you could change anything, what
would it be?

What have I learnt about:

1. Myself

2. My horse

3. My worries

4. Handling pressure

How can I use what I have learnt in
the future?

Do I need to develop more skills to put this into
place? If so what are they?

How do I now proceed and what is
the time scale?

PERFORMANCE ASSESSMENT GRID: DRESSAGE

Characteristic/skill Date:	1	2	3	4	5	6	7	8	9	10
Centre line										
Halts										
Trot left rein										
Trot right rein										
Canter left										
Canter right										
Trot circles										
Canter circles										
Transitions										

PERFORMANCE ASSESSMENT GRID: CROSS-COUNTRY

Characteristic/skill Date:	1	2	3	4	5	6	7	8	9	10
Confidence in self										
Time management										
Dressage skills										
Jumping skills										
Cross-country skills										
Handling pressure										
Competition nerves										

Index